MW01076375

Especially for

From

Date

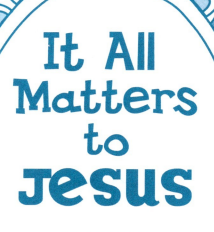

# It All Matters to Jesus

## Devotional Journal for Girls

JoAnne Simmons

BARBOUR BOOKS

An Imprint of Barbour Publishing, Inc.

## Dedication

To my parents, who raised me to know and love Jesus, and to my in-laws for doing the same for my husband. Thank you!

And to Doug and Jodi and Lilly. You make life so full of love and fun.

## Acknowledgments

Adelie, Ashley, Aubrey, Emma, Hannah, Kassadee, Sara, Sarah, and Wyndham—your honest answers were a huge help while I was writing this book. Thank you so much!

© 2019 by Barbour Publishing, Inc.

ISBN 978-1-68322-878-3

All rights reserved. No part of this publication may be reproduced or transmitted for commercial purposes, except for brief quotations in printed reviews, without written permission of the publisher.

Churches and other noncommercial interests may reproduce portions of this book without the express written permission of Barbour Publishing, provided that the text does not exceed 500 words or 5 percent of the entire book, whichever is less, and that the text is not material quoted from another publisher. When reproducing text from this book, include the following credit line: "From *It All Matters to Jesus Devotional Journal for Girls*, published by Barbour Publishing, Inc. Used by permission."

Scripture quotations marked NLT are taken from the *Holy Bible*. New Living Translation copyright© 1996, 2004, 2015 by Tyndale House Foundation. Used by permission of Tyndale House Publishers, Inc. Carol Stream, Illinois 60188. All rights reserved.

Scripture quotations marked CEV are from the Contemporary English Version, Copyright © 1995 by American Bible Society. Used by permission.

Scripture quotations marked ESV are from The Holy Bible, English Standard Version®, copyright © 2001 by Crossway Bibles, a publishing ministry of Good News Publishers. Used by permission. All rights reserved.

Scripture quotations marked NIV are taken from the HOLY BIBLE, NEW INTERNATIONAL VERSION®. NIV®. Copyright © 1973, 1978, 1984, 2011 by Biblica, Inc.™ Used by permission. All rights reserved worldwide.

Scripture quotations marked NKJV are taken from the New King James Version®. Copyright © 1982 by Thomas Nelson, Inc. Used by permission. All rights reserved.

Published by Barbour Books, an imprint of Barbour Publishing, Inc., 1810 Barbour Drive, Uhrichsville, Ohio 44683, www.barbourbooks.com

*Our mission is to inspire the world with the life-changing message of the Bible.*

Member of the
Evangelical Christian
Publishers Association

Printed in China.

06356 0318 SC

# Contents

# Introduction

Okay, first thing: stop right now, wherever you're reading this book—are you in a favorite reading spot? Is it upside down on a beanbag chair, or snuggled with a ginormous pillow on the floor, or propped up on your bed, or crammed into an empty cupboard with a flashlight? The empty cupboard was one of my favorite reading spots when I was about your age. The roof of my house was too—seriously!—but I do *not* recommend that to anyone else. I'm lucky I didn't break my neck.

Anyway, you need to get one thing straight from the start of this book: the bottom line is that YOU matter to Jesus. So *very* much so that He left a pretty posh place as God in heaven to come down to Earth as a baby, live a human life, and then suffer and die a nasty death—but rose from the dead (yay!)—all so He could make a way for you to be with Him in a perfect paradise forever. That's kind of a big deal, don't you think? And if someone loves you that much—and He totally does!—then every single thing in your life is important to Jesus as well. Mondays, manicures, mean girls. . .whatever.

If it's something that matters to you—good or bad—it matters to Jesus.

# How Much Is All—
# And How Much Does It All Matter?

Raise your hand if you like math. I'm sitting hard on my hands because I completely *don't*, but I sure hope some of you do because the world needs lots of people who are great at math.

Whether you like numbers or not, can you count to *all*?

That's like asking if you can count to infinity. You just can't do it. Well, you could try, but then you'd spend the rest of your life counting and you'd still never reach the end because (duh!) it's infinity—and who wants to count forever, no matter how much you like numbers?

The title of this book says it all matters to Jesus, emphasis on *all*. That means there is no number limit to what matters to God, and there are no limits on the types of things that matter to God.

If you're not a number lover, then maybe you're a word lover, and you like dictionaries. If you check *Merriam-Webster's* dictionary, you'll find definitions of *all* include, "the whole amount, quantity, or extent of" and "every" and "any whatever." That pretty much covers every single thing we could think of, right? There is *nothing* that matters to us that does not matter to God.

And it's not true just because it's here in this book; it's true because *God's* book, His Word, the Bible, says it's true. Check out these verses:

First Peter 5:7 (NLT) says to, "Give all your worries and cares to God, for he cares about you." Does it say just our big worries? No. It says *all*.

In the psalms we read, "Our LORD, we belong to you. We tell you what worries us, and you won't let us fall" (Psalm 55:22 CEV). We have all sorts of things that worry us, from super stressful things to things not quite so serious, but we can tell them *all* to God, and He won't let us down about them.

And no matter what, we can totally trust that "God will supply every need of yours according to his riches in glory in Christ Jesus" (Philippians 4:19 ESV). Every need, every worry, every fear, every problem, every frustration, every anger, every thought. It all matters to Jesus.

Every joy does too.

Your worries and problems aren't the only things that matter to God. The happy things in your life—joy over getting a new pet or excitement over an upcoming birthday party for a friend or an accomplishment like finally sticking that landing in gymnastics—all those types of things matter to Him as well. He wants to share in your joy, and He wants you to thank and praise Him in all things, just like these verses say:

*The LORD is my strength and shield.*
*I trust him with all my heart.*
*He helps me, and my heart is filled with joy.*
*I burst out in songs of thanksgiving.*

PSALM 28:7 NLT

. . . . . . . .

*Shout for joy to the LORD, all the earth.*
*Worship the LORD with gladness;*
*come before him with joyful songs.*

PSALM 100:1–2 NIV

. . . . . . . .

*Don't worry about anything; instead,*
*pray about everything. Tell God what you need,*
*and thank him for all he has done.*

PHILIPPIANS 4:6 NLT

*And we know that for those who love*
*God all things work together for good, for those*
*who are called according to his purpose.*

ROMANS 8:28 ESV

So, now you might be wondering how much the things in your life, good or bad, matter to God. Just a little bit? Or a lot? The best way to answer that is to focus on how much God loves you. When someone really loves you, then every single aspect of your life, big or small, matters to that person in a big way. And God sure does love you in a ginormous way. You can't ever really wrap your mind around it, actually, but you can keep coming back to the following verses about God's love, reading them and memorizing them to help you remember just how much every detail of your life matters to God.

*But God shows his love for us in that while*
*we were still sinners, Christ died for us.*

ROMANS 5:8 ESV

• • • • • • •

*For I am sure that neither death nor life, nor angels*
*nor rulers, nor things present nor things to come,*
*nor powers, nor height nor depth, nor anything else*
*in all creation, will be able to separate us from the*
*love of God in Christ Jesus our Lord.*

ROMANS 8:38–39 ESV

• • • • • • •

*For as high as the heavens are above the earth, so*
*great is his steadfast love toward those who fear him.*

PSALM 103:11 ESV

*And may you have the power to understand, as all*
*God's people should, how wide, how long, how high,*
*and how deep his love is. May you experience the love*
*of Christ, though it is too great to understand fully.*

Ephesians 3:18–19 nlt

·······

*This is real love—not that we loved God,*
*but that he loved us and sent his Son as*
*a sacrifice to take away our sins.*

1 John 4:10 nlt

·······

*How great is God's love for all who worship him?*
*Greater than the distance between heaven and earth!*

Psalm 103:11 cev

·······

*For God so loved the world that he gave his one*
*and only Son, that whoever believes in him*
*shall not perish but have eternal life.*

John 3:16 niv

And if there's any doubt left in your brain about how much God cares about any and every little detail of your life, then think about something for a moment. Do you think you could ever count all the hairs on your pretty head? They won't go to infinity, of course, but still—what a long and boring task that would be! I'm sure you can think of much more fun things to do like baking cookies with your BFF and eating gobs of chocolate chip cookie dough. (Will you save me some? Yum!)

God has done it though. He cares so much about every detail of your life that He's counted the exact number of hairs on your head.

That's pretty detailed.

You are *extremely* loved by God, and *every*thing about you matters to Him.

*Aren't two sparrows sold for only a penny?*
*But your Father knows when any one of them falls*
*to the ground. Even the hairs on your head are*
*counted. So don't be afraid! You are worth*
*much more than many sparrows.*

MATTHEW 10:29–31 CEV

 **Write About It!**

Why do you think God loves you so very much?

...........................................................................................................

...........................................................................................................

...........................................................................................................

...........................................................................................................

...........................................................................................................

...........................................................................................................

...........................................................................................................

...........................................................................................................

...........................................................................................................

...........................................................................................................

...........................................................................................................

...........................................................................................................

# IT ALL MATTERS TO JESUS

- ✿ Every worry you have matters to Jesus.
- ✿ Every problem you face matters to Jesus.
- ✿ Every fear that scares you matters to Jesus.
- ✿ Every frustration that bothers you matters to Jesus.
- ✿ Every anger you feel matters to Jesus.
- ✿ Every sorrow you suffer matters to Jesus.
- ✿ Every thought you think matters to Jesus.
- ✿ Every joy you experience matters to Jesus.
- ✿ Every accomplishment you achieve matters to Jesus.
- ✿ Even the number of hairs on your head matters to Jesus.
- ✿ .................................................................................................
- ✿ .................................................................................................
- ✿ .................................................................................................
- ✿ .................................................................................................
- ✿ .................................................................................................
- ✿ .................................................................................................
- ✿ .................................................................................................
- ✿ .................................................................................................
- ✿ .................................................................................................
- ✿ .................................................................................................

## Write About It!

What do you want to share with God today?

......................................................................................................

......................................................................................................

......................................................................................................

......................................................................................................

......................................................................................................

......................................................................................................

......................................................................................................

......................................................................................................

......................................................................................................

......................................................................................................

......................................................................................................

......................................................................................................

......................................................................................................

......................................................................................................

......................................................................................................

......................................................................................................

......................................................................................................

......................................................................................................

......................................................................................................

......................................................................................................

......................................................................................................

# Can't Live with 'Em,
# Can't Live without 'Em

It's true—your family will absolutely drive you crazy sometimes, maybe even *a lot* of the time. Sometimes we feel like we just can't live with them anymore, but we sure can't live without them either! Maybe your little brother constantly messes with your stuff—even though you've made clear it's off-limits. (Didn't he see the huge sign on your door to KEEP OUT?) Maybe your teenage sister just doesn't understand you're not trying to bother her; you just think she's super cool and you want to know all about her. (Well, okay, maybe you shouldn't have been sneaking to read all the texts on her phone.)

Maybe you don't have siblings, but your parents are always on your case about homework or music practice when you just want to chill. Maybe your parents are divorced and you're tired of shuffling back and forth and being stuck in the middle.

Or [insert your own stressful family situation here]. Maybe it's none or all of the above, but we all have ways that our family members make us want to scream. And crazy or not, they're the people in our lives who've always got our backs, the people we love the very most, the people God has purposefully placed us with.

So, does Jesus care about your family? Does He care if you fight with your siblings? Does He care that it's hard to obey your parents sometimes? Does He care about the things that cause worry and stress and pain in your family? Does He care when you're missing your cousins you only get to see on Thanksgiving? Yes, yes, yes, and yes!

God's Word says in 1 Timothy 5:8, "People who don't take care of their relatives, and especially their own families, have given up their faith. They are worse than someone who doesn't have faith in the Lord"

(CEV). Those are strong words, and they make it pretty clear how important family is to Jesus and how important our family should be to us.

So, if you have siblings, how's that going? Do you fight a little or a lot? What ways could you work harder to get along with them? Start by looking for more ways to show love and respect for them.

If a little brother wants to be in your stuff, try to find some extra time to share your things with him. He might just want some attention from you. And if your sister wants you to stop bugging her, try talking things out and telling her why she's so fascinating to you.

Things won't ever be perfect, and your siblings will hurt your feelings and you'll both pick fights at times. But look up 1 Corinthians 13 in your Bible and work harder at loving them in the way those verses talk about love. Don't get upset too easily, and be quick to forgive and forget. God will bless your efforts for trying to do things His way, living in peace and love with your family members. And remember, don't ever stop asking for His help!

Here are some more excellent verses to encourage you in getting along with your siblings:

> *Ask God to bless everyone who mistreats you. Ask him*
> *to bless them and not to curse them. When others are*
> *happy, be happy with them, and when they are sad,*
> *be sad. Be friendly with everyone. Don't be proud and*
> *feel that you are smarter than others. Make friends*
> *with ordinary people. Don't mistreat someone who*
> *has mistreated you. But try to earn the respect of*
> *others, and do your best to live at peace with everyone.*
> ROMANS 12:14–18 CEV

Now, your parents. . .how well do you get along with them? I know it sometimes seems like they never get off your back. There are so many chores and homework assignments and a bazillion times when you have to be patient or on your best behavior. You probably wonder sometimes, *Why can't I just do whatever I want?* But stop and think about all that your parents are doing for you. There's a lot of work and responsibility that goes into keeping you fed and clothed and learning and healthy and safe—and I bet you do have tons of fun in the midst of all that too, because your parents love you and want to give you nice things and good experiences. Be sure you show not just obedience and respect for your parents but love and appreciation also. The Bible has a *lot* to say about how to treat your parents. . . .

*A wise child brings joy to a father;*
*a foolish child brings grief to a mother.*

PROVERBS 10:1 NLT

* * * * * * * *

*"Each of you must show great respect*
*for your mother and father."*

LEVITICUS 19:3 NLT

* * * * * * * *

*My children, listen when your father corrects you.*
*Pay attention and learn good judgment.*

PROVERBS 4:1 NLT

* * * * * * * *

*Obey the teaching of your parents— always keep it*
*in mind and never forget it. Their teaching will guide*
*you when you walk, protect you when you sleep,*
*and talk to you when you are awake.*

PROVERBS 6:20–22 CEV

*Children with good sense accept correction from their parents, but stubborn children ignore it completely.*

PROVERBS 13:1 CEV

• • • • • • •

*Don't be a fool and disobey your parents. Be smart! Accept correction.*

PROVERBS 15:5 CEV

• • • • • • •

*"Honor your father and your mother, that your days may be long upon the land which the LORD your God is giving you."*

EXODUS 20:12 NKJV

• • • • • • •

*Pay attention to your father, and don't neglect your mother when she grows old. Invest in truth and wisdom, discipline and good sense, and don't part with them. Make your father truly happy by living right and showing sound judgment. Make your parents proud, especially your mother.*

PROVERBS 23:22–25 CEV

• • • • • • •

*Children, obey your parents in the Lord, for this is right. "Honor your father and mother" (this is the first commandment with a promise), "that it may go well with you and that you may live long in the land."*

EPHESIANS 6:1–3 ESV

Sometimes you might have a major worry for a family member—do you have a loved one who is sick? Maybe an aunt who's fighting cancer or a grandparent who has to live in a nursing home? Jesus cares so much about them, and He is working on a place for us where there will never be any more pain and sickness and suffering.

*Then I saw "a new heaven and a new earth," for the first heaven and the first earth had passed away, and there was no longer any sea. I saw the Holy City, the new Jerusalem, coming down out of heaven from God, prepared as a bride beautifully dressed for her husband. And I heard a loud voice from the throne saying, "Look! God's dwelling place is now among the people, and he will dwell with them. They will be his people, and God himself will be with them and be their God. 'He will wipe every tear from their eyes. There will be no more death' or mourning or crying or pain, for the old order of things has passed away." He who was seated on the throne said, "I am making everything new!"*

REVELATION 21:1–5 NIV

If you have a loved one who is suffering, do you know if they've accepted Jesus as their Savior? If not, think of ways you could share His love and the Gospel with them. (If you need help with this, go to page 25 on how to be sure you have Jesus as your BFF.)

**Write About It!**

How can you show more love for your family today?

............................................................................................................

............................................................................................................

# IT ALL MATTERS TO JESUS

- ❁ Your family matters to Jesus.

- ❁ Giving time and attention to a little sibling matters to Jesus.

- ❁ Respecting an older sibling's stuff and space matters to Jesus.

- ❁ Obeying your parents, even when it's hard, matters to Jesus.

- ❁ Your family members who are sick matter to Jesus.

- ❁ Your family's financial needs matter to Jesus.

- ❁ Missing your family who are far away matters to Jesus.

- ❁ Appreciating and showing love to your family matters to Jesus.

- ❁ Forgiveness matters to Jesus.

- ❁ Taking care of each other matters to Jesus.

- ❁ ....................................................................................................

- ❁ ....................................................................................................

- ❁ ....................................................................................................

- ❁ ....................................................................................................

- ❁ ....................................................................................................

- ❁ ....................................................................................................

- ❁ ....................................................................................................

- ❁ ....................................................................................................

- ❁ ....................................................................................................

# Write About It!

Who in your family needs to experience God's love in a big way?

....................................................................................................

....................................................................................................

....................................................................................................

....................................................................................................

....................................................................................................

....................................................................................................

....................................................................................................

....................................................................................................

....................................................................................................

....................................................................................................

....................................................................................................

....................................................................................................

....................................................................................................

....................................................................................................

....................................................................................................

....................................................................................................

....................................................................................................

....................................................................................................

....................................................................................................

....................................................................................................

....................................................................................................

# BFFs and Bullies and Everyone in Between

Who's your BFF? Do you have just one or a whole bunch? Or maybe you're wishing you could find one. Well, before we go any further, don't ever forget who wants to be your #1, Top of the List, Best Friend Forever—

Jesus.

Just so we have this clear, have you asked Him to be your BFF? If you haven't, do you know how? It's so simple and fantastic to accept His love and forgiveness and ask Him to be your Savior and your very best friend. If you never have, then pray a prayer like this right now:

*Dear God, I need You. I know that I mess up and do the wrong thing, but I believe Jesus died on the cross for my sins, and then He rose again and is alive right now. Please forgive me for all my mistakes and be my Savior. Please be my best friend forever and help me to follow You! Thank You for loving me and helping me. Thank You that everything about me matters to You. In Jesus' name, amen.*

(Check out these scriptures to help you understand—John 3:16; Romans 3:23; Romans 6:23; Romans 5:8; Romans 10:9–10.)

When Jesus is your BFF, He wants to help you in all your other friendships too. Have you had a fight with a friend recently? Has someone you thought was a good friend been ignoring you lately? Has a friend started acting so differently that you're not even sure you want to be friends anymore? Has a close friend moved away and you miss her terribly?

All these things matter to Jesus.

Or maybe you're blessed and nothing is going wrong with your friends right now, and you are thrilled to have one awesome BFF or maybe more than one! Great! Jesus wants us to have good friends, get along them, love them, and live in peace with them. Check out these verses from His Word:

*A friend loves at all times.*

PROVERBS 17:17 NIV

• • • • • • •

*There are "friends" who destroy each other,*
*but a real friend sticks closer than a brother.*

PROVERBS 18:24 NLT

• • • • • • •

*The heartfelt counsel of a friend is as*
*sweet as perfume and incense.*

PROVERBS 27:9 NLT

• • • • • • •

*Two are better than one, because they have a good*
*return for their labor: If either of them falls down,*
*one can help the other up. But pity anyone who falls*
*and has no one to help them up. Also, if two lie down*
*together, they will keep warm. But how can one keep*
*warm alone? Though one may be overpowered,*
*two can defend themselves. A cord of three*
*strands is not quickly broken.*

ECCLESIASTES 4:9–12 NIV

*As iron sharpens iron, so a friend sharpens a friend.*

PROVERBS 27:17 NLT

Unfortunately, things do go wrong with friends sometimes because we're all human and none of us is perfect—no matter how much we wish that we were.

Sometimes friends will make you feel left out and lonely. When that happens, talk it out with a parent or other trusted grown-up and see if there are ways you can work it out with that friend. And always remember that God has said, "Never will I leave you; never will I forsake you" (Hebrews 13:5 NIV). If there are times where you feel left out by friends, use that time to get closer to God. Let Him show you how much He loves you by spending extra time reading your Bible and listening to music that praises Him. You can also use the time to find ways to help others more, and you might be surprised at how God brings new friends into your life.

If you're not being left out, be thankful, and be careful not to leave someone else out. Be sensitive to ways that other friends feel, and find ways to include them if you think they're feeling like an outsider, whether it's at school or at church or on the playground or during a dance class or a team sport.

Do you feel like your friends are always getting you into trouble or pressuring you to do things that you know you shouldn't? Are there boys wanting to be more than just friends or other girls pressuring you to be more than just friends with a boy? Then here's the deal: you absolutely need to make some new friends and let the troublemakers go.

The Bible says in 1 Corinthians 15:33, "Don't fool yourselves. Bad friends will destroy you" (CEV).

And in Proverbs 13:20 it says, "Wise friends make you wise, but you hurt yourself by going around with fools" (CEV).

Do you have friends who pick on you or tease too much—or maybe they're not friends at all but downright bullies? Don't ever be afraid to get help from a parent, teacher, or other trusted grown-up in cases like this (no matter how much the bully threatens to make you miserable if you do), and remember that God sees and knows the hurt done to you. His Word says this:

> *Never take revenge. Leave that to the righteous anger of God. For the Scriptures say, "I will take revenge; I will pay them back," says the LORD. Instead, "If your enemies are hungry, feed them. If they are thirsty, give them something to drink. In doing this, you will heap burning coals of shame on their heads." Don't let evil conquer you, but conquer evil by doing good.*
>
> ROMANS 12:19–21 NLT

Sometimes you've done the best you can and a friend still hurts or betrays you or bullies you too much—and you finally just have to let them go. Jesus knows these things will happen. He cares about your hurts, and He cares about your knowing that He is the one true friend who will never let you down.

With Jesus as your Savior, remember your purpose here on earth is to live in relationship with Him and share His love. Do your best to be loving and kind to everyone who comes into your life, for whatever time you get to count them as a friend, confident that nothing and no one can ever take away your greatest friend of all—Jesus.

> *God loves you and has chosen you as his own special people. So be gentle, kind, humble, meek, and patient. Put up with each other, and forgive anyone who does you wrong, just as Christ has*

*forgiven you. Love is more important than anything else. It is what ties everything completely together.*

Colossians 3:12–14 CEV

## How can you be a better friend?

........................................................................................

........................................................................................

........................................................................................

........................................................................................

........................................................................................

........................................................................................

........................................................................................

........................................................................................

........................................................................................

........................................................................................

........................................................................................

........................................................................................

........................................................................................

........................................................................................

........................................................................................

........................................................................................

# IT ALL MATTERS TO JESUS

❀ Being your #1, top-of-the-list BFF matters to Jesus.

❀ Having good friends matters to Jesus.

❀ Staying away from troublesome friends matters to Jesus.

❀ When you feel left out, it matters to Jesus.

❀ Including others and being a good friend matters to Jesus.

❀ When you feel bullied, it matters to Jesus.

❀ When you lose a friend, it matters to Jesus.

❀ Being kind to those who are unkind to you matters to Jesus.

❀ Not seeking revenge matters to Jesus.

❀ Drawing closer to Him when you feel alone matters to Jesus.

❀ ......................................................................................................

❀ ......................................................................................................

❀ ......................................................................................................

❀ ......................................................................................................

❀ ......................................................................................................

❀ ......................................................................................................

❀ ......................................................................................................

❀ ......................................................................................................

❀ ......................................................................................................

❀ ......................................................................................................

# Write About It!

Have you ever been bullied? How did you handle it?

........................................................................................................
........................................................................................................
........................................................................................................
........................................................................................................
........................................................................................................
........................................................................................................
........................................................................................................
........................................................................................................
........................................................................................................
........................................................................................................
........................................................................................................
........................................................................................................
........................................................................................................
........................................................................................................
........................................................................................................
........................................................................................................
........................................................................................................
........................................................................................................
........................................................................................................
........................................................................................................
........................................................................................................
........................................................................................................
........................................................................................................
........................................................................................................

# Everything You're Thinking About

Isn't it incredible that God knows *everything*? Especially that He knows your every thought. How can He keep track of the thoughts of so many people in the world? It's kind of mind-boggling, huh? But it's true! Read this beautiful psalm:

*You have looked deep into my heart, Lord,*
*and you know all about me. You know when*
*I am resting or when I am working, and from*
*heaven you discover my thoughts.*

*You notice everything I do and everywhere I go.*
*Before I even speak a word, you know what I will*
*say, and with your powerful arm you protect me*
*from every side. I can't understand all of this!*
*Such wonderful knowledge is far above me.*

*Where could I go to escape from your Spirit or*
*from your sight? If I were to climb up to the highest*
*heavens, you would be there. If I were to dig down*
*to the world of the dead you would also be there.*

*Suppose I had wings like the dawning day and flew*
*across the ocean. Even then your powerful*
*arm would guide and protect me. Or suppose I said,*
*"I'll hide in the dark until night comes to cover me*
*over." But you see in the dark because daylight*
*and dark are all the same to you.*

*You are the one who put me together inside my*
*mother's body, and I praise you because of the*

*wonderful way you created me. Everything you*
*do is marvelous! Of this I have no doubt.*

*Nothing about me is hidden from you! I was secretly*
*woven together deep in the earth below, but with*
*your own eyes you saw my body being formed.*
*Even before I was born, you had written in*
*your book everything I would do.*

*Your thoughts are far beyond my understanding,*
*much more than I could ever imagine. I try*
*to count your thoughts, but they outnumber*
*the grains of sand on the beach.*

PSALM 139:1–18 CEV

Wow! Isn't it awesome that the God of the universe knows you so well and loves you so much?

Since God knows everything about you, even the thoughts that you think, they obviously matter to Him—and it should matter to you whether your thoughts please Him or not. Here's what the Bible says to think about:

*And now, dear brothers and sisters, one final thing.*
*Fix your thoughts on what is true, and honorable,*
*and right, and pure, and lovely, and admirable. Think*
*about things that are excellent and worthy of praise.*

PHILIPPIANS 4:8 NLT

Let's stop and do a little brain scan—you'll need some aluminum foil, a lightbulb, and some electrical wire. . .just kidding. We'll leave that kind of thing to the doctors and scientists, and I'm pretty sure they use much more sophisticated equipment.

Seriously though, do your thoughts match up with that scripture?

Hopefully a lot of the time they do, but probably not always. It's tough to always think positively, especially when so many things are going wrong all around you, and especially when you forget that God is listening to your thoughts. The good news is, you can train your brain to do better.

Every time your thoughts start to stray toward things that are false or negative or sinful or hateful or full of complaining, you can think of this verse and ask God to help you focus on good things—like the Truth in His Word, the ways He has helped you in the past, the blessings in your life, the promises of God, and His SUPERSIZED love for you!

One verse that's so easy to memorize and so very helpful for training your brain is Isaiah 26:3—"You will keep in perfect peace all who trust in you, all whose thoughts are fixed on you!" (NLT).

Picture your favorite animal at the zoo. Now picture it going totally nuts-o when a zookeeper tries to settle it into its new exhibit. Wild, right?

Your thoughts don't have to be untamable, like a wild animal that can't be controlled. You can choose to train your brain not to dwell on the bad but focus on the good. This doesn't mean you have to pretend the hard things don't exist. You don't have to step out of reality when bad things happen. But you can learn to never let those negatives take over your head!

Here are some more great verses to help you choose good thoughts:

*Let God change the way you think.*
*Then you will know how to do everything*
*that is good and pleasing to him.*

ROMANS 12:2 CEV

. . . . . . .

*Think about the things of heaven,*
*not the things of earth.*

COLOSSIANS 3:2 NLT

*"Love the Lord your God with all your heart and with all your soul and with all your mind."*

MATTHEW 22:37 ESV

. . . . . . .

*Let the Spirit change your way of thinking.*

EPHESIANS 4:23 CEV

. . . . . . .

*Let my words and my thoughts be pleasing to you, LORD, because you are my mighty rock and my protector.*

PSALM 19:14 CEV

Do your parents ever tell you to watch your attitude or that you need an attitude adjustment? Your thoughts are what shape your attitude, and your attitude matters to Jesus.

What would your reaction be to this scenario: You've been looking forward all week to a Friday night out with just your mom and your BFF to see a new movie you've been waiting on FOR.EV.ER. But then your baby sister gets sick and is vomiting all over the house, and your mom cancels on your friend and the movie.

Ugh! You can choose to think about how bummed you are, how disgusting vomit is, how you're going to have to help clean up the mess and probably get sick too, how everything is always about the baby, and how unfair life is. And all those thoughts are going to make your attitude just as stinky as all the puke—and probably get you into trouble with your parents if you add a bad attitude to an already tough situation.

Or you could say, "Yep, this is a bummer." It's fine to admit it! But then you can choose to think good thoughts—how much you love your baby sister and you're sorry she got sick, how much you love your mom and that she'd appreciate a cheerful helper cleaning up all the puke mess, and how there's always another weekend where you can plan a fun movie night with a friend. And that will make your attitude a good one, which pleases God. . .and will likely earn you some bonus points with your parents. Win, win, win!

## Write About It!

When was the last time you had a stinky attitude?
How did you turn it around?

...................................................................................................................

...................................................................................................................

...................................................................................................................

...................................................................................................................

...................................................................................................................

...................................................................................................................

...................................................................................................................

...................................................................................................................

...................................................................................................................

...................................................................................................................

...................................................................................................................

...................................................................................................................

...................................................................................................................

...................................................................................................................

...................................................................................................................

# IT ALL MATTERS TO JESUS

- ❀ Thinking about what is true matters to Jesus.

- ❀ Thinking about what is honorable matters to Jesus.

- ❀ Thinking about what is right matters to Jesus.

- ❀ Thinking about what is pure matters to Jesus.

- ❀ Thinking about what is lovely matters to Jesus.

- ❀ Thinking about what is admirable matters to Jesus.

- ❀ Thinking about things that are excellent and worthy of praise matters to Jesus.

- ❀ Keeping your thoughts fixed on God and His promises matters to Jesus.

- ❀ Your attitude toward a disappointing situation matters to Jesus.

- ❀ Training your brain to refocus when you are thinking negatively matters to Jesus.

- ❀ ......................................................................................

- ❀ ......................................................................................

- ❀ ......................................................................................

- ❀ ......................................................................................

- ❀ ......................................................................................

- ❀ ......................................................................................

- ❀ ......................................................................................

# Write About It!

How does it feel to know that God knows all your thoughts?

# What Goes In

Do you have a grandma or maybe another older loved one to make warm, fuzzy memories with? I sure hope so. A favorite memory I have of my "Mema," who is now in heaven, is of a song she used to sing with me called "Oh Be Careful Little Eyes." If you were to Google it right now, you might roll your eyes at the old-fashioned music videos you'll find, but the message of it is still relevant and valuable, a reminder that what you see and hear matters to Jesus.

Another song I remember that I used to listen to on these crazy old things called cassette tapes (ask your mom and dad about them) was called the "Computer Song" that went like this: "Input, output, what goes in is what comes out. Input, output, that is what it's all about. Input, output, your mind is a computer whose input, output, daily you must choose."

Catchy, huh? LOL!

The point is, what you feed your brain and your heart—the things you watch on TV and the internet, the types of books and magazines and blogs you read, the Facebook posts and tweets you follow, the type of music you listen to, the video games you play—might just seem like harmless entertainment and socializing, but they are much more than that. They totally affect what comes out of you too. They affect your beliefs and your words and your attitudes and your actions. And everything that "goes in" matters *a lot* to Jesus. He wants you to fill yourself up with good stuff.

Check out these verses:

> *Your eyes are the lamp for your body. When your eyes are good, you have all the light you need. But when your eyes are bad, everything is dark. So be sure*

*that your light isn't darkness. If you have light, and*
*nothing is dark, then light will be everywhere, as when*
*a lamp shines brightly on you.*

LUKE 11:34–36 CEV

• • • • • • •

*I will not look with approval on anything that is vile.*
*I hate what faithless people do; I will have no part in*
*it. The perverse of heart shall be far from me;*
*I will have nothing to do with what is evil.*

PSALM 101:3–4 NIV

• • • • • • •

*Put everything to the test. Accept what is good*
*and don't have anything to do with evil.*

1 THESSALONIANS 5:21–22 CEV

• • • • • • •

*I pray that God, who gives peace, will make you*
*completely holy. And may your spirit, soul, and body*
*be kept healthy and faultless until our Lord Jesus*
*Christ returns.*

1 THESSALONIANS 5:23 CEV

• • • • • • •

*"Bad company corrupts good character." Think*
*carefully about what is right, and stop sinning.*

1 CORINTHIANS 15:33–34 NLT

So, what should you put in? First off, fill yourself up with God's Word. Spend time in it, not just at church or Sunday school but *daily*. It's our guidebook for life, and it's our map to make our way closer and closer to Jesus until we can be with Him forever.

Here are some awesome verses to encourage you to study and memorize and live by God's Word:

*All Scripture is breathed out by God and profitable for teaching, for reproof, for correction, and for training in righteousness, that the man of God may be complete, equipped for every good work.*

2 Timothy 3:16–17 esv

* * * * * * *

*"This Book of the Law shall not depart from your mouth, but you shall meditate on it day and night, so that you may be careful to do according to all that is written in it. For then you will make your way prosperous, and then you will have good success."*

Joshua 1:8 esv

* * * * * * *

*And the Scriptures were written to teach and encourage us by giving us hope.*

Romans 15:4 cev

* * * * * * *

*For the word of God is alive and powerful. It is sharper than the sharpest two-edged sword, cutting between soul and spirit, between joint and marrow. It exposes our innermost thoughts and desires.*

Hebrews 4:12 nlt

* * * * * * *

*Your word is a lamp for my feet, a light on my path.*

Psalm 119:105 niv

*With my whole heart I seek you; let me not wander
from your commandments! I have stored up your
word in my heart, that I might not sin against you.*

PSALM 119:10–11 ESV

. . . . . . . .

*Heaven and earth will pass away,
but my words will not pass away.*

MATTHEW 24:35 ESV

I'm not saying that if you like a popular non-Christian song on the radio, it's always a bad thing, or that every single book you read has to have a Christian message. You don't have to be out of touch with the reality of the world around you or watch only religious movies and TV and can't ever enjoy a song that doesn't have lyrics about God. My point is, what are you continually filling your mind with, and what are you letting affect you and your actions and testimony as a Christian?

Remember the verse we looked at earlier?

*Finally, my friends, keep your minds on whatever
is true, pure, right, holy, friendly, and proper.
Don't ever stop thinking about what is
truly worthwhile and worthy of praise.*

PHILIPPIANS 4:8 CEV

Here's the deal—if your heart is full of God's Word and you are walking closely to Jesus, you simply have to ask Him to help you be careful and smart about the movies, TV, books, music, etc., that you put into your life. And when you have the Holy Spirit in you, He will help you be attracted to what is good for you and avoid what is bad for you.

Keep this verse as a guide:

*Let the message about Christ, in all its richness,*
*fill your lives. Teach and counsel each other with all*
*the wisdom he gives. Sing psalms and hymns and*
*spiritual songs to God with thankful hearts.*
*And whatever you do or say, do it as a*
*representative of the Lord Jesus, giving thanks*
*through him to God the Father.*

COLOSSIANS 3:16–17 NLT

Fill your brain and your heart and your life up with Jesus and His Word, and remember that everything that goes into your head and your heart matters to Him.

Do you think God really does care about what
you watch on the screen? Why?

........................................................................................

........................................................................................

........................................................................................

........................................................................................

........................................................................................

........................................................................................

........................................................................................

........................................................................................

# IT ALL MATTERS TO JESUS

- ❀ The music you listen to matters to Jesus.

- ❀ The books you read matter to Jesus.

- ❀ The websites you visit matter to Jesus.

- ❀ The magazines you read matter to Jesus.

- ❀ The blogs you read matter to Jesus.

- ❀ The movies you watch matter to Jesus.

- ❀ The TV shows you watch matter to Jesus.

- ❀ Everything you put into your head and your heart matters to Jesus.

- ❀ Asking for God's help in choosing what to put in your mind matters to Jesus.

- ❀ Filling up on God's Word matters to Jesus.

- ❀ .............................................................................................

- ❀ .............................................................................................

- ❀ .............................................................................................

- ❀ .............................................................................................

- ❀ .............................................................................................

- ❀ .............................................................................................

- ❀ .............................................................................................

- ❀ .............................................................................................

# What Comes Out—Your Words

It's a big deal when a baby starts talking. Have you asked your mom or dad what your firsts few words were? Were you a quiet toddler or a little chatterbox? Your parents might have recorded videos from when you first started talking and other fun times when you were smaller. Maybe you can plan a home movie night sometime where the star of the show is you! (Don't forget the popcorn!)

Our words are always a big deal to Jesus. Look at this scripture:

*All of us do many wrong things. But if you can control your tongue, you are mature and able to control your whole body. By putting a bit into the mouth of a horse, we can turn the horse in different directions. It takes strong winds to move a large sailing ship, but the captain uses only a small rudder to make it go in any direction. Our tongues are small too, and yet they brag about big things. It takes only a spark to start a forest fire! The tongue is like a spark. It is an evil power that dirties the rest of the body and sets a person's entire life on fire with flames that come from hell itself. All kinds of animals, birds, reptiles, and sea creatures can be tamed and have been tamed. But our tongues get out of control. They are restless and evil, and always spreading deadly poison. My dear friends, with our tongues we speak both praises and curses. We praise our Lord and Father, and we curse people who were created to be like God, and this isn't right.*

JAMES 3:2–10 CEV

There's so much to ponder in those verses, but the bottom line is that your words are very powerful. They can do a lot of good, and they can do a lot of bad—and they are very hard to control.

Think about how easy it is to say disrespectful things to your parents or quickly respond with "no"—and then all of a sudden you're in trouble for disobeying. Or how often you "vent" in frustration, and suddenly all these ugly words are coming out of your mouth. Or when a sibling or friend upsets you and in no time you're yelling hateful and hurtful words. Our words are so tied to what we're feeling—mad, sad, frustrated, whatever—and we often let them spew without thinking. The emotions come and go, but the words will be remembered.

Do yourself a huge favor while you are young and get in the super-smart habit of controlling what you say. I'm guessing you don't like to be called immature, right? Do you know a way you can start being really mature (more mature than many, many grown-ups I know)? Start learning to be "quick to hear, slow to speak, slow to anger" (James 1:19 ESV). Not only will you be more mature; you will find and keep truer friends and have better relationships with them and your family.

*The tongue can bring death or life;*
*those who love to talk will reap the consequences.*

PROVERBS 18:21 NLT

• • • • • • •

*A kind answer soothes angry feelings, but harsh*
*words stir them up. Words of wisdom come from*
*the wise, but fools speak foolishness. The LORD sees*
*everything, whether good or bad. Kind words are*
*good medicine, but deceitful words can really hurt.*

PROVERBS 15:1–4 CEV

*Sharp words cut like a sword,*
*but words of wisdom heal.*

PROVERBS 12:18 CEV

• • • • • ••

*Keep your tongue from speaking evil*
*and your lips from telling lies!*

PSALM 34:13 NLT

• • • • • ••

*"Do you really love life? Do you want to be happy?*
*Then stop saying cruel things and quit telling lies."*

1 PETER 3:10 CEV

• • • • • ••

*"The food that you put into your mouth doesn't make*
*you unclean and unfit to worship God. The bad*
*words that come out of your mouth are*
*what make you unclean."*

MATTHEW 15:11 CEV

• • • • • ••

*Let my words and my thoughts be pleasing to you,*
*LORD, because you are my mighty rock*
*and my protector.*

PSALM 19:14 CEV

• • • • • ••

*You will be well rewarded for saying something*
*kind, but all some people think about*
*is how to be cruel and mean.*

PROVERBS 13:2 CEV

*Watching what you say can save you a lot of trouble.*

PROVERBS 21:23 CEV

Your written words matter too, whether it's in your diary or journal, or in emails, texts, and social media sites like Facebook and Twitter. Don't forget all these scriptures when you're communicating in these ways, being especially careful because when your words are written down and maybe sent over the internet, they're very easy for someone to copy and potentially use against you. It's very smart to follow the Bible's advice:

*Don't use foul or abusive language. Let everything
you say be good and helpful, so that your words will be
an encouragement to those who hear them.*

EPHESIANS 4:29 NLT

It's a huge challenge to watch carefully over our words. You will make mistakes at times, but keep this as your prayer:

*Take control of what I say, O LORD, and guard my lips.*

PSALM 141:3 NLT

Jesus will always be so happy to help you!

**Write About It!**

Has anyone ever spoken hurtful words to you?
If so, how did it make you feel?

...................................................................................................

...................................................................................................

# IT ALL MATTERS TO JESUS

- ❀ Everything you say, speak, or write matters to Jesus.

- ❀ What you say to your parents matters to Jesus.

- ❀ What you say to your siblings matters to Jesus.

- ❀ What you say to your friends matters to Jesus.

- ❀ What you say to your teachers and youth leaders matters to Jesus.

- ❀ What you say on social media matters to Jesus.

- ❀ What you write in your blog or journal matters to Jesus.

- ❀ Being quick to listen, slow to speak, and slow to become angry matters to Jesus.

- ❀ Being able to control your words matters to Jesus.

- ❀ Being encouraging, kind, and helpful with your words matters to Jesus.

- ❀ .........................................................................................

- ❀ .........................................................................................

- ❀ .........................................................................................

- ❀ .........................................................................................

- ❀ .........................................................................................

- ❀ .........................................................................................

- ❀ .........................................................................................

- ❀ .........................................................................................

# What Comes Out—Your Actions

Have you ever had a classmate or known someone at Sunday school who acts sugary sweet and obedient when the teacher is watching, and as soon as the teacher turns around, they're mean or they're trying to cheat off your paper or they're breaking all the rules? They're sort of like that creepy old story of Dr. Jekyll and Mr. Hyde. It's so frustrating!

And, unfortunately, there are all sorts of religious leaders and grown-ups in our world today who say one thing and act another—they pretend to love and follow Jesus and the Bible, but if someone looks closer into how they live their lives. . .things start looking weird. . . things just don't add up.

People who continuously act like this are called hypocrites, and it matters a lot to Jesus that we do not act like hypocrites. It matters to Jesus that our "what comes out" matches our "what goes in" about Him. How we act as Christians should line up with what we say about our faith in Jesus, and what we say about Him should match what His Word says is true about Him.

There are a lot of strong verses in the Bible that talk about hypocrites:

*"Not everyone who calls me their Lord will get into the kingdom of heaven. Only the ones who obey my Father in heaven will get in. On the day of judgment many will call me their Lord. They will say, "We preached in your name, and in your name we forced out demons and worked many miracles." But I will tell them, "I will have nothing to do with you! Get out of my sight, you evil people!"*

MATTHEW 7:21–23 CEV

*"You hypocrites! Isaiah was right when he prophesied about you, for he wrote, 'These people honor me with their lips, but their hearts are far from me. Their worship is a farce, for they teach man-made ideas as commands from God.' "*

MATTHEW 15:7–9 NLT

• • • • • • •

*Whoever says "I know him" but does not keep his commandments is a liar, and the truth is not in him.*

1 JOHN 2:4 ESV

• • • • • • •

*Whoever says he is in the light and hates his brother is still in darkness.*

1 JOHN 2:9 ESV

• • • • • • •

*If anyone says, "I love God," and hates his brother, he is a liar; for he who does not love his brother whom he has seen cannot love God whom he has not seen.*

1 JOHN 4:20 ESV

• • • • • • •

*My friends, what good is it to say you have faith, when you don't do anything to show that you really do have faith? Can that kind of faith save you? If you know someone who doesn't have any clothes or food, you shouldn't just say, "I hope all goes well for you. I hope you will be warm and have plenty to eat." What good is it to say this, unless you do something to help? Faith that doesn't lead us to do good deeds is all alone and dead!*

*Suppose someone disagrees and says, "It is possible to have faith without doing kind deeds."*

*I would answer, "Prove that you have faith without doing kind deeds, and I will prove that I have faith by doing them." You surely believe there is only one God. That's fine. Even demons believe this, and it makes them shake with fear.*

JAMES 2:14–19 CEV

• • • • • • •

*If we say we have fellowship with him while we walk in darkness, we lie and do not practice the truth.*

1 JOHN 1:6 ESV

I'm sure you've heard the old saying that "actions speak louder than words." It's absolutely true. Be careful that the way you live your life and the way you treat others matches up with what you say about loving Jesus. Mostly, if you say you love Jesus, your actions will overflow with obedience to His Word and boundless love for others. Being a "Doer of the Word" matters *so much* to Jesus.

*But be doers of the word, and not hearers only, deceiving yourselves. For if anyone is a hearer of the word and not a doer, he is like a man who looks intently at his natural face in a mirror. For he looks at himself and goes away and at once forgets what he was like. But the one who looks into the perfect law, the law of liberty, and perseveres, being no hearer who forgets but a doer who acts, he will be blessed in his doing.*

JAMES 1:22–25 ESV

# Write About It!

Do your actions show that you are a Jesus-follower?

# IT ALL MATTERS TO JESUS

- ✿ Everything you do matters to Jesus.

- ✿ *Not* being a hypocrite matters to Jesus.

- ✿ Matching what you do to what you say matters to Jesus.

- ✿ Not just saying but *showing* that you are a Christian matters to Jesus.

- ✿ Obeying God and His Word matters to Jesus.

- ✿ Proving your faith by your good deeds matters to Jesus.

- ✿ Loving others matters to Jesus.

- ✿ Being doers, not just hearers, of the Word matters to Jesus.

- ✿ ...................................................................................................

- ✿ ...................................................................................................

- ✿ ...................................................................................................

- ✿ ...................................................................................................

- ✿ ...................................................................................................

- ✿ ...................................................................................................

- ✿ ...................................................................................................

- ✿ ...................................................................................................

- ✿ ...................................................................................................

- ✿ ...................................................................................................

- ✿ ...................................................................................................

# Write About It!

How can you shine your light for Jesus today?

........................................................................................

........................................................................................

........................................................................................

........................................................................................

........................................................................................

........................................................................................

........................................................................................

........................................................................................

........................................................................................

........................................................................................

........................................................................................

........................................................................................

........................................................................................

........................................................................................

........................................................................................

........................................................................................

........................................................................................

........................................................................................

........................................................................................

........................................................................................

........................................................................................

........................................................................................

........................................................................................

# Color with Love

Do you still like to color? I do! I especially love a brand-new box of crayons or markers. And there are so many fun kinds these days. Twistable crayons, glittery crayons, water-color paint crayons...so many super cool options to create a beautiful work of art.

Imagine that you could wake up every morning and see outlined coloring-book pages of your day, kind of like a black-and-white comic strip. Now imagine picking out the love-colored crayon (whatever color that looks like to you!) and shading in each picture. That's what Jesus wants us to do, to color everything we do, every day we have on this earth with love. Love matters to Him so much, and by loving others, we share His love. He said in John 13:34–35, "A new commandment I give to you, that you love one another: just as I have loved you, you also are to love one another. By this all people will know that you are my disciples, if you have love for one another" (ESV).

Here are just a handful of scenarios of ways you can color your day with love:

When you get a good grade on a test, it's great to be happy, but you can also be humble and not flaunt it or brag about it in any of your classmates' faces, especially some who might not have done well.

*Let all that you do be done in love.*

1 CORINTHIANS 16:14 ESV

When your sibling picks a fight with you, either do your best to work it out and be a peacemaker or walk away until you can get a parent or other grown-up to help.

*Put on then, as God's chosen ones, holy and beloved,*
*compassionate hearts, kindness, humility, meekness,*
*and patience, bearing with one another and, if one*
*has a complaint against another, forgiving each*
*other; as the Lord has forgiven you, so you also must*
*forgive. And above all these put on love, which binds*
*everything together in perfect harmony.*

COLOSSIANS 3:12–14 ESV

When it's unfair that Mom promised to take you to the mall, but the car broke down, offer her love and understanding that you can reschedule for another time.

*Above all, love each other deeply, because*
*love covers over a multitude of sins.*

1 PETER 4:8 NIV

When you're so frustrated that Dad promised to shoot hoops with you, but he had to work late three nights in a row at a very stressful job, instead of being upset find a way to encourage him.

*Always be humble and gentle. Patiently put*
*up with each other and love each other.*

EPHESIANS 4:2 CEV

When you see Mom and Dad are extra tired, help make supper, set the table, and look for little chores that need to be done without being asked.

*Dear children, let us not love with words or*
*speech but with actions and in truth.*

1 JOHN 3:18 NIV

When you are blessed with a special treat, share it with a friend or sibling.

*May the Lord make your love for each other and for*
*everyone else grow by leaps and bounds.*
1 Thessalonians 3:12 cev

When you see a friend in Sunday school who feels shy and left out, invite them into your circle of friends.

*One of the teachers of religious law was standing*
*there listening to the debate. He realized that*
*Jesus had answered well, so he asked, "Of all the*
*commandments, which is the most important?" Jesus*
*replied, "The most important commandment is this:*
*'Listen, O Israel! The Lord our God is the one and only*
*Lord. And you must love the Lord your God with all*
*your heart, all your soul, all your mind, and all your*
*strength.' The second is equally important:*
*'Love your neighbor as yourself.' No other*
*commandment is greater than these."*
Mark 12:28–31 nlt

When a classmate is acting mean to you, share your dessert with her at lunchtime.

*"Love your enemies! Do good to them. Lend to them*
*without expecting to be repaid. Then your reward*
*from heaven will be very great, and you will truly be*
*acting as children of the Most High, for he is kind to*
*those who are unthankful and wicked. You must be*

*compassionate, just as your*
*Father is compassionate."*

LUKE 6:35–36 NLT

Some of the most famous love verses of the Bible are found in 1 Corinthians 13. They describe what true love looks like, the way we should strive to love everyone around us all the time:

*What if I could speak all languages of humans*
*and of angels? If I did not love others, I would be*
*nothing more than a noisy gong or a clanging*
*cymbal. What if I could prophesy and understand*
*all secrets and all knowledge? And what if I had faith*
*that moved mountains? I would be nothing, unless*
*I loved others. What if I gave away all that I owned*
*and let myself be burned alive? I would gain nothing,*
*unless I loved others. Love is kind and patient, never*
*jealous, boastful, proud, or rude. Love isn't selfish or*
*quick tempered. It doesn't keep a record of wrongs*
*that others do. Love rejoices in the truth, but not in*
*evil. Love is always supportive, loyal, hopeful,*
*and trusting. Love never fails!*

1 CORINTHIANS 13:1–8 CEV

You might wonder, if I'm doing all these loving things, what good is it for me? Who's going to be showing love for me? You will be amazed at the return on your investment. Loving others makes you incredibly loveable. Not only will other people see your love and want to return it, but God especially sees, and He will bless you and fill your heart to bursting with satisfaction and joy. Loving is what God made us for!

*My dear friends, we must love each other. Love comes*
*from God, and when we love each other, it shows*
*that we have been given new life. We are now God's*
*children, and we know him. God is love, and anyone*
*who doesn't love others has never known him. God*
*showed his love for us when he sent his only Son into*
*the world to give us life. Real love isn't our love for*
*God, but his love for us. God sent his Son to be the*
*sacrifice by which our sins are forgiven. Dear friends,*
*since God loved us this much, we must love each other.*
*No one has ever seen God. But if we love each other,*
*God lives in us, and his love is truly in our hearts.*

1 JOHN 4:7–12 CEV

**Write About It!**

In what ways do you color the world with love?

...................................................................................................................

...................................................................................................................

...................................................................................................................

...................................................................................................................

...................................................................................................................

...................................................................................................................

...................................................................................................................

...................................................................................................................

...................................................................................................................

65

# IT ALL MATTERS TO JESUS

- ❁ Loving your parents matters to Jesus.
- ❁ Loving your siblings matters to Jesus.
- ❁ Loving your friends matters to Jesus.
- ❁ Loving your enemies matters to Jesus.
- ❁ Letting love color everything you do matters to Jesus.
- ❁ .............................................................................................
- ❁ .............................................................................................
- ❁ .............................................................................................
- ❁ .............................................................................................
- ❁ .............................................................................................
- ❁ .............................................................................................
- ❁ .............................................................................................
- ❁ .............................................................................................
- ❁ .............................................................................................
- ❁ .............................................................................................
- ❁ .............................................................................................
- ❁ .............................................................................................
- ❁ .............................................................................................
- ❁ .............................................................................................
- ❁ .............................................................................................

# Write About It!

## Who needs your love today?

---

---

---

---

---

---

---

---

---

---

---

---

---

---

---

---

---

---

# The Truth, the Whole Truth, and Nothing but the Truth

Think about a time when a friend lied to you. Did you like it? Did it make it hard to trust her again?

Now think about a time when you lied to your parents and were caught. What were the consequences? Was it worth it?

Here is just a little of what the Bible says about lying:

*Do not tell lies about others.*

Exodus 20:16 CEV

• • • • • • •

*Don't lie to each other, for you have stripped off your old sinful nature and all its wicked deeds.*

Colossians 3:9 NLT

• • • • • • •

*The Lord detests lying lips, but he delights in those who tell the truth.*

Proverbs 12:22 NLT

• • • • • • •

*A false witness will not go unpunished, and a liar will be destroyed.*

Proverbs 19:9 NLT

• • • • • • •

*Therefore each of you must put off falsehood and speak truthfully to your neighbor.*

Ephesians 4:25 NIV

*If you do the right thing, honesty will be your guide.*
*But if you are crooked, you will be trapped*
*by your own dishonesty.*

PROVERBS 11:3 CEV

Unfortunately, lying is so common these days. It's hard to find the truth sometimes, so it's incredibly important that those of us who love and follow Jesus stand strong in the truth—about everything!

It might seem like "little white lies" and bending the truth when we need to are no big deal, but they are! Because if you start out willing to lie about little things, then at some point you're likely willing to lie about big things.

People who aren't totally committed to living honest lives end up being people who can't really be trusted with much of anything.

Do you want to be a person whom others can trust? Do you want your parents and teachers and leaders at church to give you important tasks and responsibilities, knowing that you'll follow through on them? Do you want to have friends who feel safe telling you anything at all because they know you won't blab it around where it doesn't need to be told? Or do you want to be the girl whom grown-ups know they have to keep a constant eye on and have to question everything she's doing? Or the one that other girls are afraid to talk to because she spreads so much gossip?

*"If you are faithful in little things, you will be faithful*
*in large ones. But if you are dishonest in little things,*
*you won't be honest with greater responsibilities. And*
*if you are untrustworthy about worldly wealth, who*
*will trust you with the true riches of heaven? And if*
*you are not faithful with other people's things, why*
*should you be trusted with things of your own?"*

LUKE 16:10–12 NLT

If you don't want to be *that* girl who can't be trusted (who ends up being that grown-up with all kinds of problems), then start now being honest in Every. Single. Thing. You. Do.

Tell the truth, even if there are consequences. (Believe me, the consequences won't be as bad if you're honest about the problem.) Have integrity. Proverbs 10:9 (ESV) says, "Whoever walks in integrity walks securely, but he who makes his ways crooked will be found out." And Proverbs 19:1 (ESV) says, "Better is a poor person who walks in his integrity than one who is crooked in speech and is a fool."

Follow through when you make a commitment. If there are circumstances beyond your control that make it impossible to keep a commitment, then give a heads-up to whomever you're reporting to. Be consistent about doing what you say you will do. You've heard guys say, "I'm a man of my word." Well, you should strive to be a girl of your word—who will end up becoming an awesome woman of your word!

And never forget why we tell the truth and what we base our truth on—Jesus Himself.

*Jesus answered, "I am the way and the truth and the life. No one comes to the Father except through me."*
JOHN 14:6 NIV

If you are leading an honest life, always telling the truth, you will help others come to know Jesus as the Way, the Truth, and the Life.

If you have messed up and lied, then go and make it right with God, knowing that, "If we confess our sins, he is faithful and just and will forgive us our sins and purify us from all unrighteousness" (1 John 1:9 NIV).

# Write About It!

Why is it so important to always tell the truth?

........................................................................................
........................................................................................
........................................................................................
........................................................................................
........................................................................................
........................................................................................
........................................................................................
........................................................................................
........................................................................................
........................................................................................
........................................................................................
........................................................................................
........................................................................................
........................................................................................
........................................................................................
........................................................................................
........................................................................................
........................................................................................
........................................................................................
........................................................................................

# IT ALL MATTERS TO JESUS

- ❁ Telling the truth matters to Jesus.
- ❁ Having integrity matters to Jesus.
- ❁ Keeping commitments matters to Jesus.
- ❁ Being able to be trusted with a little matters to Jesus.
- ❁ Being able to be trusted with a lot matters to Jesus.
- ❁ ......................................................................................
- ❁ ......................................................................................
- ❁ ......................................................................................
- ❁ ......................................................................................
- ❁ ......................................................................................
- ❁ ......................................................................................
- ❁ ......................................................................................
- ❁ ......................................................................................
- ❁ ......................................................................................
- ❁ ......................................................................................
- ❁ ......................................................................................
- ❁ ......................................................................................
- ❁ ......................................................................................
- ❁ ......................................................................................
- ❁ ......................................................................................

# Write About It!

Have you ever told a lie? What were the consequences?

# Heartbreak

What's the saddest thing that you've ever experienced? Has a close friend moved away? Have your parents gotten divorced? Has a favorite pet died? Have you lost a loved one to cancer or a car accident? Maybe you're blessed that none of these have happened to you, but you've watched and tried to comfort a friend or family member who has gone through them. Because of sin, our broken world is so full of hurt and sadness that it just seems completely overwhelming at times.

Among other terrible hurts, I've held my favorite pet in my arms as they gave him the shot to put him to sleep—and I was completely heartbroken. I held my grandpa's hand and heard him struggle for every breath as he lay dying of cancer—and I was completely heartbroken.

I'm sure you've been heartbroken in some way before too.

The bright spot in our saddest circumstances is this promise from the Bible: "The LORD is close to the brokenhearted; he rescues those whose spirits are crushed" (Psalm 34:18 NLT).

When your heart is breaking, don't ever forget that He hasn't left you. He has promised, "Never will I leave you; never will I forsake you" (Hebrews 13:5 NIV). Maybe you don't feel like it. Maybe you feel like He's forgotten you or you can't understand how or why awful things happen to good people. But in those moments, you have a choice to turn away from God because you're mad at Him, or you can choose to draw closer to Him and trust Him despite your hurt—and let Him comfort you and help you through the dark, sad days. Little by little they *will* get better. His Word says, "Come close to God, and God will come close to you" (James 4:8 NLT). And "The LORD is near to all who call on him, to all who call on him in truth" (Psalm 145:18 ESV).

When life is at its worst, the worst thing you can do is run from God. If you stick it out and stay close to Him, He will carry you through it.

And remember that because Jesus rose from the grave, He defeated sin and death, and we have awesome hope and confidence that one day all the hurt in this world will end, and we will never, ever be sad again. These verses from 1 Peter 1:3–7 (CEV), are so encouraging:

*Praise God, the Father of our Lord Jesus Christ. God is so good, and by raising Jesus from death, he has given us new life and a hope that lives on. God has something stored up for you in heaven, where it will never decay or be ruined or disappear. You have faith in God, whose power will protect you until the last day. Then he will save you, just as he has always planned to do. On that day you will be glad, even if you have to go through many hard trials for a while. Your faith will be like gold that has been tested in a fire. And these trials will prove that your faith is worth much more than gold that can be destroyed. They will show that you will be given praise and honor and glory when Jesus Christ returns.*

No matter how sad you are or how bad life hurts you, don't ever give up! We "live by faith, not by what we see" (2 Corinthians 5:7 CEV), and our faith is in a living Savior and in a place where all things will be made right someday—heaven, where "God will make his home among his people. He will wipe all tears from their eyes, and there will be no more death, suffering, crying, or pain" (Revelation 21:3–4 CEV).

*We can rejoice, too, when we run into problems and trials, for we know that they help us develop endurance. And endurance develops strength of*

*character, and character strengthens our confident*
*hope of salvation. And this hope will not lead to*
*disappointment. For we know how dearly God loves*
*us, because he has given us the Holy Spirit*
*to fill our hearts with his love.*

ROMANS 5:3–5 NLT

 Write About It!

What kinds of things break your heart?

# IT ALL MATTERS TO JESUS

❀ All your hurts matter to Jesus.

❀ If a friend breaks your heart, it matters to Jesus.

❀ If you're hurting over your parents' divorce, it matters to Jesus.

❀ If a loved one dies, it matters to Jesus.

❀ If you have to put a favorite pet to sleep, it matters to Jesus.

❀ Drawing close to Him when you are hurting matters to Jesus.

❀ Trusting Him when you are hurting matters to Jesus.

❀ Not giving up when you are hurting matters to Jesus.

❀ .................................................................................

❀ .................................................................................

❀ .................................................................................

❀ .................................................................................

❀ .................................................................................

❀ .................................................................................

❀ .................................................................................

❀ .................................................................................

❀ .................................................................................

❀ .................................................................................

❀ .................................................................................

## Write About It!

How does knowing Jesus help soothe your hurts?

........................................................................................................
........................................................................................................
........................................................................................................
........................................................................................................
........................................................................................................
........................................................................................................
........................................................................................................
........................................................................................................
........................................................................................................
........................................................................................................
........................................................................................................
........................................................................................................
........................................................................................................
........................................................................................................
........................................................................................................
........................................................................................................
........................................................................................................
........................................................................................................
........................................................................................................
........................................................................................................
........................................................................................................
........................................................................................................
........................................................................................................

# In the Mirror

How much time do you spend in front of the mirror? Are you a girl who likes to take awhile getting your hair just right, or would you rather throw it in a ponytail and be done? Do you like pretty jewelry and accessories to match your outfits, or could you not care less about that kind of stuff? Do you like skirts and dresses or jeans and T-shirts? Or maybe it just depends on your mood?

No matter if you wear sparkly barrettes and headbands that perfectly coordinate with your clothes every day or if you use the same simple ponytail holder with any outfit because it always matches, Jesus cares about looks—but not in the way the world cares. Our culture likes to make us think we have to have the latest fashions, huge bright eyes, and perfect hair to be beautiful. But Jesus cares what your heart looks like, and if your heart is beautiful, then your beauty shines brighter than any model on any magazine cover. The Bible says, "People judge by outward appearance, but the LORD looks at the heart" (1 Samuel 16:7 NLT).

And what's He looking for in your heart?

First off, it matters if your heart has had a Jesus makeover, meaning you believe in Him and have asked Him to be your Savior and Lord over your life. It's incredible to think that Jesus died and became the sacrifice for our sin so that God, who is so good and holy, can look at us and not see our ugly sin, but He sees us as righteous, just like it says in 1 Corinthians 1:30 (NLT): "Christ made us right with God; he made us pure and holy, and he freed us from sin." And in 2 Corinthians 5:21 (NLT): "For God made Christ, who never sinned, to be the offering for our sin, so that we could be made right with God through Christ."

I hope you are incredibly thankful for that! I hope it gives you goose bumps or makes you want to cry happy tears!

It seems like you could just stop there, doesn't it? If Jesus already did the work of forgiving your sins and you accept that and God sees you as righteous, then it's all good, everything is beautiful, and you can live your life any way you want because everything is forgiven. But here's the deal: a *true* relationship with Jesus is active, and it never stops seeking God and His will for your life. God made you for a purpose! He sees you as so beautiful when you are doing the things He planned for you to do.

Ephesians 2:10 (NIV) says, "For we are God's handiwork, created in Christ Jesus to do good works, which God prepared in advance for us to do."

Don't ever stop asking God what those good works are that He has for you to do, and don't ever stop praying and reading His Word to find out.

Here are a couple more verses on God's idea of beautiful—which should be our idea of beautiful:

> *Don't be concerned about the outward beauty of*
> *fancy hairstyles, expensive jewelry, or beautiful*
> *clothes. You should clothe yourselves instead with*
> *the beauty that comes from within, the unfading*
> *beauty of a gentle and quiet spirit, which is so*
> *precious to God.*
>
> 1 PETER 3:3–4 NLT

· · · · · · ··

> *Charm can be deceiving, and beauty fades away,*
> *but a woman who honors the LORD deserves to*
> *be praised. Show her respect—praise her in public*
> *for what she has done.*
>
> PROVERBS 31:30–31 CEV

The bottom line is, true beauty comes from within, from a spirit that is gentle and quietly seeking God and honoring Him in every area of life. If you are doing those things, you can't help but shine the stunning light of Jesus and real beauty to everyone around you.

What about physical fitness and perfectly tan and toned bodies? Our culture sure puts a lot of emphasis on how amazing those things are. Being healthy certainly is great, and God wants us to take good care of our bodies. He even says that our bodies are a temple: "Do you not know that your bodies are temples of the Holy Spirit, who is in you, whom you have received from God? You are not your own; you were bought at a price. Therefore honor God with your bodies" (1 Corinthians 6:19–20 NIV).

But we should never be obsessed with physical fitness, as so many in our world are today. It seems like too many people are one extreme or the other—either they have no desire to truly care for their bodies, or they are consumed with making sure they eat exactly the right foods and exercise in exactly the right way so that every muscle is in exactly the right condition. Neither of those is right. What's right is a healthy balance, and this verse sums it up perfectly:

*For physical training is of some value, but godliness has value for all things, holding promise for both the present life and the life to come.*

1 TIMOTHY 4:8 NIV

Keeping our bodies healthy matters for this life so that we can actually do the good works God has planned for us to do, but eventually these earthly bodies of ours will wear out. So godly fitness—keeping our spirits and minds and hearts healthy by training them in God's Word and with prayer and with serving others and going to church—is what has value for forever in heaven.

So, does Jesus care that you're upset when you're having a hideous hair day? Or if you have a ginormous bruise on your face from playing softball and it's picture day at school? Absolutely! He cares in that He loves you and wants to help you through those hard things, but nothing like that ever means you are less beautiful to Him. And when you are beautiful to the Creator God of the universe, who is the King of all kings, then think about this—does it really matter at all who else thinks you are beautiful or not? You are to God, and that is always enough!

## Write About It!

How can people be beautiful on the inside?

........................................................................................................................

........................................................................................................................

........................................................................................................................

........................................................................................................................

........................................................................................................................

........................................................................................................................

........................................................................................................................

........................................................................................................................

........................................................................................................................

........................................................................................................................

........................................................................................................................

........................................................................................................................

# IT ALL MATTERS TO JESUS

- Being beautiful on the inside matters to Jesus.

- It's the heart, not the outward looks, that matters most to Jesus.

- Having a Jesus makeover, letting Him get rid of your ugly sin, matters to Jesus.

- Physical fitness matters to Jesus, but godly fitness matters more.

- Gentle and quiet spirits matter to Jesus.

- Honoring the Lord matters to Jesus.

- ................................................................................

- ................................................................................

- ................................................................................

- ................................................................................

- ................................................................................

- ................................................................................

- ................................................................................

- ................................................................................

- ................................................................................

- ................................................................................

- ................................................................................

- ................................................................................

# Write About It!

What makes you beautiful?

........................................................................................

........................................................................................

........................................................................................

........................................................................................

........................................................................................

........................................................................................

........................................................................................

........................................................................................

........................................................................................

........................................................................................

........................................................................................

........................................................................................

........................................................................................

........................................................................................

........................................................................................

........................................................................................

........................................................................................

........................................................................................

........................................................................................

........................................................................................

# Gimmie, Gimmie, Gimmie!

It's funny how if you watch commercials on TV or look at ads online or catalogs from the mail, you start thinking you just have to have the latest toys, games, shoes, and clothes. Everything looks so cool, doesn't it? It kinda makes you want to say, "Gimmie, gimmie, gimmie!" Have you been begging your parents for anything lately? Is there a particular gift you're hoping for on your birthday or Christmas?

It's not bad to want some nice things, and giving us good gifts matters to Jesus. He gave us the best gift ever, after all—Himself, as the Savior of our sins, and He's preparing a ginormous gift of a forever home in heaven with Him.

Here is some of what the Bible has to say about God's best gift to us:

*You were saved by faith in God, who treats us much better than we deserve. This is God's gift to you, and not anything you have done on your own. It isn't something you have earned, so there is nothing you can brag about.*

Ephesians 2:8–9 CEV

• • • • • • •

*All have sinned and fall short of the glory of God, and are justified by his grace as a gift, through the redemption that is in Christ Jesus.*

Romans 3:23–24 ESV

• • • • • • •

*Thank God for his gift that is too wonderful for words!*

2 Corinthians 9:15 CEV

On top of the best gift of all, God is giving us gifts along the way too in our daily lives. Look at these verses:

> *"You parents—if your children ask for a loaf of bread, do you give them a stone instead? Or if they ask for a fish, do you give them a snake? Of course not! So if you sinful people know how to give good gifts to your children, how much more will your heavenly Father give good gifts to those who ask him."*
>
> MATTHEW 7:9–11 NLT

. . . . . . .

> *Whatever is good and perfect is a gift coming down to us from God our Father, who created all the lights in the heavens. He never changes or casts a shifting shadow.*
>
> JAMES 1:17 NLT

Sometimes you receive a gift that you don't really want. Do you like getting plain white socks for Christmas? Or toothpaste in your stocking? Those aren't that fun. But they *are* things that you need.

It's important to learn when you are very young the difference between needs and wants. And it's important to be thankful for receiving the things that you need and realizing that sometimes getting the things you want is just an awesome added bonus!

We don't need the latest fashions, but we do need warm clothes, and God promises to provide them:

> *"Look at the lilies and how they grow. They don't work or make their clothing, yet Solomon in all his glory was not dressed as beautifully as they are. And if God cares so wonderfully for flowers that are here*

*today and thrown into the fire tomorrow,*
*he will certainly care for you."*

LUKE 12:27–28 NLT

We don't need gourmet meals or to eat at restaurants all the time, but we do need healthy foods, and God will make sure we have them:

*"And don't be concerned about what to eat and what*
*to drink. Don't worry about such things. These things*
*dominate the thoughts of unbelievers all over the*
*world, but your Father already knows your needs."*

LUKE 12:29–30 NLT

When Jesus teaches us to pray in the Bible, He says, "Give us this day our daily bread" (Matthew 6:11 NKJV). He doesn't add this to the prayer: "And I need doughnuts for tomorrow and bagels and cream cheese, and milk to go with, and then maybe a cookie. And what are we going to eat the day after that?" No. He says *daily bread*, meaning simply what we need to keep us going each day, without worrying about the next day or the day after that.

We need to focus on how rich we are, without *stuff*. As Christians we are called to "seek the Kingdom of God above all else, and live righteously, and he will give you everything you need " (Matthew 6:33 NLT). That means our purpose should not be to pile up stuff that we can't take with us when we die, but to focus on God and obeying Him and letting Him provide everything we need.

The Bible also says to "take delight in the LORD, and he will give you the desires of your heart" (Psalm 37:4 NIV). Does that mean that as long as you are happy with God, then He will get you those new shoes you're drooling over, or that new iPod or bike or game or whatever? Sometimes maybe, just as an added bonus, but mostly it means when your happiness is focused on God, He will be changing your heart so that you constantly find your joy and satisfy your desires by just knowing and serving and loving Him.

## Write About It!

What is the best gift you have ever received and why?

........................................................................................

........................................................................................

........................................................................................

........................................................................................

........................................................................................

........................................................................................

........................................................................................

........................................................................................

........................................................................................

........................................................................................

........................................................................................

........................................................................................

........................................................................................

........................................................................................

........................................................................................

........................................................................................

........................................................................................

........................................................................................

# IT ALL MATTERS TO JESUS

❀ Your wants matter to Jesus.

❀ Your needs matter more to Jesus.

❀ Learning the difference between wants and needs matters to Jesus.

❀ Realizing that all good gifts come from God matters to Jesus.

❀ Being thankful for gifts (even socks and toothpaste!) matters to Jesus.

❀ Seeking God first, before *stuff*, matters to Jesus.

❀ Finding your happiness in Him rather than stuff matters to Jesus.

❀ ......................................................................................................................

❀ ......................................................................................................................

❀ ......................................................................................................................

❀ ......................................................................................................................

❀ ......................................................................................................................

❀ ......................................................................................................................

❀ ......................................................................................................................

❀ ......................................................................................................................

❀ ......................................................................................................................

❀ ......................................................................................................................

# From Pet Peeves to Seeing Red

Do you have a pet peeve—something common that bothers you? Like someone squeezing the toothpaste tube from the middle rather than the bottom. Toilet paper under instead of over, or the opposite. People cutting in line. When someone tries to talk to you when you're reading. When your mom asks you to hurry up and get ready to go "RIGHT! NOW!" but then you wait in the car for what seems like forever while *she* finishes getting ready.

Ugh! Those things can make you irritated, but what makes you *really angry*? Or as some people describe it, what makes you see red? (Picture those funny characters on old cartoons, with their faces colored crimson and steam coming from their ears!) Do your friends ever cause drama over nothing? Do your parents punish you too quickly before listening to your side sometimes? Have you been lied to? Gossiped about? Maybe even things much worse than this. . . .

But the Bible tells us to be very careful with anger:

*Control your temper, for anger labels you a fool.*

ECCLESIASTES 7:9 NLT

• • • • • ••

*Fools vent their anger, but the wise quietly hold it back.*

PROVERBS 29:11 NLT

• • • • • ••

*A kind answer soothes angry feelings,*
*but harsh words stir them up.*

PROVERBS 15:1 CEV

*Good sense makes one slow to anger,*
*and it is his glory to overlook an offense.*

PROVERBS 19:11 ESV

• • • • • • •

*The LORD is merciful and gracious,*
*slow to anger and abounding in steadfast love.*

PSALM 103:8 ESV

• • • • • • •

*Stop being bitter and angry and mad at others. Don't*
*yell at one another or curse each other or ever be rude.*
*Instead, be kind and merciful, and forgive others, just*
*as God forgave you because of Christ.*

EPHESIANS 4:31–32 CEV

• • • • • • •

*You must quit being angry, hateful, and evil.*
*You must no longer say insulting or*
*cruel things about others.*

COLOSSIANS 3:8 CEV

It's a seriously messed-up world that we live in. Unfortunately there are lots of things that are going to make you angry in your life. *Lots* of things. It is okay, even good, to be angry sometimes. The Bible actually *says* to be angry:

*Be angry, and do not sin; ponder in your own hearts*
*on your beds, and be silent. Offer right sacrifices, and*
*put your trust in the LORD.*

PSALM 4:4–5 ESV

*Be angry and do not sin; do not let the sun go down on*
*your anger, and give no opportunity to the devil.*

Ephesians 4:26–27 esv

But it's extremely important for you to control how quickly you become angry and how you react in your anger:

*Be patient and trust the Lord. Don't let it bother you*
*when all goes well for those who do sinful things.*
*Don't be angry or furious. Anger can lead to sin.*

Psalm 37:7–8 cev

• • • • • • •

*Understand this, my dear brothers and sisters: You*
*must all be quick to listen, slow to speak, and slow*
*to get angry. Human anger does not produce the*
*righteousness God desires.*

James 1:19–20 nlt

Basically, we should not dive headfirst straight into the deep end of anger when something goes wrong. And when we are angry, we cannot use that as an excuse to sin. Did you notice that both of those verses that said "be angry" also said "do not sin"?

Even when seriously unfair and horrible stuff has been done to us, we are not supposed to retaliate or "get even." The Bible says:

*Dear friends, don't try to get even. Let God take*
*revenge. In the Scriptures the Lord says, "I am the one*
*to take revenge and pay them back." The Scriptures*
*also say, "If your enemies are hungry, give them*
*something to eat. And if they are thirsty, give them*
*something to drink. This will be the same as piling*

*burning coals on their heads." Don't let evil*
*defeat you, but defeat evil with good.*

ROMANS 12:19–21 CEV

We have to control ourselves and do our very best not to sin. In other words, if your little sister pours a bottle of bubbles all over the art project you just spent twelve hours on, it's not wrong of you to feel angry. That would totally stink! But it's not okay to be so angry that you go break her favorite toy to get even.

If a classmate cheats off your paper and gets you both in trouble, it's okay to be mad. It's not okay to snatch her homework and tear it up the next day. When you feel the emotion of anger, you need to slow it down, not let it overcome you. Count to ten or even one hundred, run to your bedroom and cry into your pillow, whatever calming action helps you take a little time-out to get your feelings under control. Most of all, ask God to help you deal with it in the right way. Ask Him to calm you down and give you wisdom on how to get help and make things right.

And admit it, sometimes you get really angry over stuff that truly is not a big deal. We all do. When we're feeling tired, impatient, and/or stressed out, sometimes the things that maybe should be a little pet peeve make us freak and lash out with really angry words and/or actions. When that happens, you need to make it right. You need to apologize and ask forgiveness from the person you acted out on, and you need to take it to God for His forgiveness and for His help to deal with it better in the future. It's truly an ongoing challenge, but one that Jesus will always help you with—because how you deal with anger matters so much to Him.

# Write About It!

## What helps to calm your anger?

# IT ALL MATTERS TO JESUS

❀ Being slow to get angry matters to Jesus.

❀ When you do feel angry, controlling it matters to Jesus.

❀ Letting God do the "getting even" matters to Jesus.

❀ Apologizing when you've acted in anger matters to Jesus.

❀ Choosing kind words instead of angry words matters to Jesus.

❀ .............................................................................

❀ .............................................................................

❀ .............................................................................

❀ .............................................................................

❀ .............................................................................

❀ .............................................................................

❀ .............................................................................

❀ .............................................................................

❀ .............................................................................

❀ .............................................................................

❀ .............................................................................

❀ .............................................................................

❀ .............................................................................

❀ .............................................................................

# Flying Monkeys and Other Fears

Do you like the classic movie *The Wizard of Oz*? I love it, but when I was little, I was scared of the Wicked Witch of the West—and I was completely *terrified* of her flying monkeys! They were so creepy! I vividly remember hiding behind the couch when they came on the screen and having a couple of nightmares about them. Now I can look back and laugh about that, but I still have fears. Everyone does, no matter what age you are. Our fears just change a bit with each year we grow older and with each new life experience we have.

I don't want to write a list of things you might be scared of, in case I mention one you haven't thought of and it becomes a new fear for you. That wouldn't be very nice of me! I'm sure it's not hard for you to think of things that make you scared, the things that keep you awake at night or keep you from doing the things you'd like to do. But you just need to know that God is bigger than every single one of your fears, and He wants to take them from you and give you peace about them.

There are so many encouraging scriptures that you can read to help you with your fears. The best thing you can do to conquer your fears is to memorize verses to fight them, and when you feel the fear creeping up on you, keep saying the verse over and over and let God's power and peace conquer that fear!

*Fear not, for I am with you;*
*be not dismayed, for I am your God;*
*I will strengthen you, I will help you,*
*I will uphold you with my righteous right hand.*
ISAIAH 41:10 ESV

*Don't worry about anything; instead, pray about
everything. Tell God what you need, and thank him
for all he has done. Then you will experience God's
peace, which exceeds anything we can understand.
His peace will guard your hearts and
minds as you live in Christ Jesus.*

PHILIPPIANS 4:6–7 NLT

• • • • • • •

*When I am afraid, I put my trust in you.*

PSALM 56:3 ESV

• • • • • • •

*For God gave us a spirit not of fear but of power and
love and self-control.*

2 TIMOTHY 1:7 ESV

• • • • • • •

*"Be strong and courageous. Do not fear or be in dread
of them, for it is the LORD your God who goes with you.
He will not leave you or forsake you."*

DEUTERONOMY 31:6 ESV

• • • • • • •

*I asked the LORD for help, and he saved
me from all my fears.*

PSALM 34:4 CEV

• • • • • • •

*"Have I not commanded you? Be strong and courageous.
Do not be afraid; do not be discouraged, for the LORD
your God will be with you wherever you go."*

JOSHUA 1:9 NIV

*Say to those with fearful hearts,*
*"Be strong, and do not fear, for your God is*
*coming to destroy your enemies.*
*He is coming to save you."*

ISAIAH 35:4 NLT

• • • • • •

*"I am leaving you with a gift—peace of mind and*
*heart. And the peace I give is a gift the world cannot*
*give. So don't be troubled or afraid."*

JOHN 14:27 NLT

• • • • • •

*No, in all these things we are more than conquerors*
*through him who loved us. For I am convinced that*
*neither death nor life, neither angels nor demons,*
*neither the present nor the future, nor any powers,*
*neither height nor depth, nor anything else in all*
*creation, will be able to separate us from the love of*
*God that is in Christ Jesus our Lord.*

ROMANS 8:37–39 NIV

• • • • • •

*Now, who will want to harm you if you are eager to do*
*good? But even if you suffer for doing what is right,*
*God will reward you for it. So don't worry or be afraid*
*of their threats. Instead, you must worship*
*Christ as Lord of your life.*

1 PETER 3:13–15 NLT

*Even though I walk through the valley of the shadow of death, I will fear no evil, for you are with me; your rod and your staff, they comfort me.*

PSALM 23:4 ESV

• • • • • • •

*The LORD is my light and my salvation—whom shall I fear? The LORD is the stronghold of my life— of whom shall I be afraid?*

PSALM 27:1 NIV

• • • • • • •

*The LORD is on my side; I will not fear. What can man do to me?*

PSALM 118:6 ESV

• • • • • • •

*God is our refuge and strength, always ready to help in times of trouble. So we will not fear when earthquakes come and the mountains crumble into the sea. Let the oceans roar and foam. Let the mountains tremble as the waters surge!*

PSALM 46:1–3 NLT

• • • • • • •

*My enemies chase me all day. Many of them are pursuing and attacking me, but even when I am afraid, I keep on trusting you. I praise your promises! I trust you and am not afraid. No one can harm me.*

PSALM 56:1–4 CEV

## Write About It!

When you are afraid, what gives you courage?

.......................................................................................................................

.......................................................................................................................

.......................................................................................................................

.......................................................................................................................

.......................................................................................................................

.......................................................................................................................

.......................................................................................................................

.......................................................................................................................

.......................................................................................................................

.......................................................................................................................

.......................................................................................................................

.......................................................................................................................

.......................................................................................................................

.......................................................................................................................

.......................................................................................................................

.......................................................................................................................

.......................................................................................................................

.......................................................................................................................

.......................................................................................................................

.......................................................................................................................

.......................................................................................................................

.......................................................................................................................

# IT ALL MATTERS TO JESUS

- ✿ Your big fears matter to Jesus.
- ✿ Your little fears matter to Jesus.
- ✿ Praying when you are afraid matters to Jesus.
- ✿ Trusting in God when you are afraid matters to Jesus.
- ✿ Memorizing scripture to fight fear matters to Jesus.
- ✿ Knowing that God is on your side matters to Jesus.
- ✿ Helping others who are afraid matters to Jesus.
- ✿ ....................................................................................
- ✿ ....................................................................................
- ✿ ....................................................................................
- ✿ ....................................................................................
- ✿ ....................................................................................
- ✿ ....................................................................................
- ✿ ....................................................................................
- ✿ ....................................................................................
- ✿ ....................................................................................
- ✿ ....................................................................................
- ✿ ....................................................................................
- ✿ ....................................................................................
- ✿ ....................................................................................

# Live and Learn

It's amazing and awesome how many options there are these days for different ways of doing school. Public schools, private schools, charter schools, homeschool, e-schools, just to name a few. There's even something called un-schooling! There are so many different ways for any type of learner to get a good education and fit the type of lifestyle that you and your family have.

So, how do you do school? Are you happy with it, or do you wish you were able to do something different? Do you enjoy school or just kind of suffer through it? Are you eager to learn and work hard, or do all the assignments and studying seem like such a drag? Do you like to learn in traditional ways or do you need to do things in a totally unique way?

There are positives and negatives about each different kind of school. There are good days and bad with any kind. There are some assignments and subjects we have to force ourselves to get through and others that we love to do! Whether you're mostly happy with school or not, your attitude toward it matters to Jesus.

The Bible says, "Whatever you do, work at it with all your heart, as working for the Lord" (Colossians 3:23 NIV). *Whatever you do*, yes even the math assignments that make you crazy or the daily reading assignments that take forever or the science fair project that seems so overwhelming. And the parts that you love or are super easy for you, do those with your whole heart too! God wants you to give your very best effort to doing your work well. Think of turning in each assignment not just to your teacher but to the God of the universe, the Creator of all learning, who loves you more than anyone else does! When you do your best with a good attitude, you show the excellence He has created you for, which brings Him praise and honor and ends up showing His light and love to those around you.

Here is some of what the Bible has to say about learning:

*Do you see someone skilled in their work?*
*They will serve before kings; they will not serve*
*before officials of low rank.*

PROVERBS 22:29 NIV

. . . . . . .

*Commit yourself to instruction;*
*listen carefully to words of knowledge.*

PROVERBS 23:12 NLT

. . . . . . .

*Commit your work to the LORD,*
*and your plans will be established.*

PROVERBS 16:3 ESV

. . . . . . .

*Intelligent people are always ready to learn.*
*Their ears are open for knowledge.*

PROVERBS 18:15 NLT

. . . . . . .

*If you have good sense, you will learn all you can,*
*but foolish talk will soon destroy you.*

PROVERBS 10:14 CEV

. . . . . . .

*If you have good sense, instruction will help you*
*to have even better sense. And if you live right,*
*education will help you to know even more.*

PROVERBS 9:9 CEV

Better and more important than any book knowledge or high test scores or college degrees, though, is this command:

> *Respect and obey the LORD! This is the*
> *beginning of wisdom. To have understanding,*
> *you must know the Holy God.*
>
> PROVERBS 9:10 CEV

Respecting and obeying the Lord, or fearing Him as some versions of this verse put it, is the starting point for any real wisdom. A person could grow up learning in the very best schools, getting the highest grades and test scores, and the best degree in college. They could have all the worldly smarts you can think of, but if they don't know and obey and respect God, then all that is for nothing in the end, and they don't have true wisdom.

As you're living and learning and growing up, you also need to be very careful to compare every new thing you learn to God's Word. Many people in the world will try to tell you the Bible is not true and that believing in Jesus and living a Christian life is silly. They'll have lots of convincing sounding evidence to back up their talk too. But when you are tested in that way, remember the following verses, keep yourself closely walking with God, ask Christian grown-ups to help you with the questions you have, stay involved in a Bible-teaching church, and ask God to show you more and more of His truth.

> *Above all, you must realize that no prophecy*
> *in Scripture ever came from the prophet's own*
> *understanding, or from human initiative.*
> *No, those prophets were moved by the Holy*
> *Spirit, and they spoke from God.*
>
> 2 PETER 1:20–21 NLT

*And we also thank God continually because, when you received the word of God, which you heard from us, you accepted it not as a human word, but as it actually is, the word of God, which is indeed at work in you who believe.*

1 THESSALONIANS 2:13 NIV

• • • • • ••

*For the word of God is living and active, sharper than any two-edged sword, piercing to the division of soul and of spirit, of joints and of marrow, and discerning the thoughts and intentions of the heart.*

HEBREWS 4:12 ESV

• • • • • ••

*Just as you accepted Christ Jesus as your Lord, you must continue to follow him. Let your roots grow down into him, and let your lives be built on him. Then your faith will grow strong in the truth you were taught, and you will overflow with thankfulness. Don't let anyone capture you with empty philosophies and high-sounding nonsense that come from human thinking and from the spiritual powers of this world, rather than from Christ.*

COLOSSIANS 2:6–8 NLT

# Write About It!

What do you love to learn about most?

.......................................................................................
.......................................................................................
.......................................................................................
.......................................................................................
.......................................................................................
.......................................................................................
.......................................................................................
.......................................................................................
.......................................................................................
.......................................................................................
.......................................................................................
.......................................................................................
.......................................................................................
.......................................................................................
.......................................................................................
.......................................................................................
.......................................................................................
.......................................................................................
.......................................................................................
.......................................................................................

# IT ALL MATTERS TO JESUS

- Your education matters to Jesus.

- Doing your best on your schoolwork matters to Jesus.

- Comparing everything you learn to the Bible matters to Jesus.

- Learning at a Bible-teaching church matters to Jesus.

- Your good days at school matter to Jesus.

- Your bad days at school matter to Jesus.

- Fearing God matters to Jesus.

- Gaining wisdom matters to Jesus.

- ......................................................................................................

- ......................................................................................................

- ......................................................................................................

- ......................................................................................................

- ......................................................................................................

- ......................................................................................................

- ......................................................................................................

- ......................................................................................................

- ......................................................................................................

- ......................................................................................................

- ......................................................................................................

## Write About It!

Do you work to memorize God's Word?
If so, what's your favorite memory verse and why?

..............................................................................................................

..............................................................................................................

..............................................................................................................

..............................................................................................................

..............................................................................................................

..............................................................................................................

..............................................................................................................

..............................................................................................................

..............................................................................................................

..............................................................................................................

..............................................................................................................

..............................................................................................................

..............................................................................................................

..............................................................................................................

..............................................................................................................

..............................................................................................................

..............................................................................................................

..............................................................................................................

..............................................................................................................

..............................................................................................................

# Busyness and Breathers

What are your favorite things to do with your time? Hang out with friends? Dance? Gymnastics? Soccer? Art? Reading? Music? Running? Video games? Crafts? Board games? Movies? With church and school and homework and activities and family and friends, there doesn't seem to be enough hours in the day! Oh, and what about sleep? Sleep needs to fit in there somewhere. And these days, everyone seems to be so busy—All. The. Time. Busy can be good, and busy can be bad—and it matters to Jesus how we spend our time.

Maybe you've heard someone in church talk about being a Mary type of person or a Martha type of person. In the Bible in Luke chapter 10, Jesus had a talk with a woman named Martha about being too busy to just relax and spend time listening to Him and learning from Him, like her sister Mary was doing. And here's the thing, Martha wasn't doing bad things with her time, she was doing *good* things—serving others and being a great hostess—but even the good things that keep us busy turn into bad ways to spend our time IF they are keeping us from spending time with Jesus.

*Now as they went on their way, Jesus entered a village. And a woman named Martha welcomed him into her house. And she had a sister called Mary, who sat at the Lord's feet and listened to his teaching. But Martha was distracted with much serving. And she went up to him and said, "Lord, do you not care that my sister has left me to serve alone? Tell her then to help me." But the Lord answered her, "Martha, Martha, you are anxious and troubled about many things, but one thing is necessary. Mary has*

*chosen the good portion, which will*
*not be taken away from her."*

It's ginormously important to get in the habit now while you're young of making daily quiet time with Jesus. It matters so much to Him. Imagine if you have a friend who calls you her BFF and yet never talks to you, never listens to you, never sets aside any time to hang out with you. That's not much of a friend at all, is it? If you call Jesus your friend and Savior, make sure you are spending daily time with Him—*quiet* time as you pray and read His Word, so that you can learn to hear from Him.

Be wise and purposeful with your time, remembering that good things can turn into bad things if you don't focus on what's really important. For example, you can spend all kinds of time in church activities and helping with ministries. . .but never spend any time actually talking to and listening to God and reading your Bible. And which is more important?

You can spend all kinds of time doing activities with your friends, but have no time to actually *be* a friend by listening to, praying with, or keeping someone company who needs you. And which is more important?

You can spend hours at your desk trying to get your homework done. . .but your mind keeps wandering or you keep playing on your iPod and wasting your time. And which is more important?

Check out these verses on using time, and ask God to help you spend every minute of your precious time wisely:

*Look carefully then how you walk, not as unwise but*
*as wise, making the best use of the time, because*
*the days are evil. Therefore do not be foolish,*

*but understand what the will of the Lord is.*

EPHESIANS 5:15–17 ESV

· · · · · · ·

*"This is what the LORD of Heaven's Armies says: Look at what's happening to you! You have planted much but harvest little. You eat but are not satisfied. You drink but are still thirsty. You put on clothes but cannot keep warm. Your wages disappear as though you were putting them in pockets filled with holes!*
*"This is what the LORD of Heaven's Armies says: Look at what's happening to you! Now go up into the hills, bring down timber, and rebuild my house. Then I will take pleasure in it and be honored, says the LORD.*
*You hoped for rich harvests, but they were poor. And when you brought your harvest home, I blew it away. Why? Because my house lies in ruins, says the LORD of Heaven's Armies, while all of you are busy building your own fine houses."*

HAGGAI 1:5–9 NLT

We need to spend our time doing things that will matter for eternity, not just for this life, because like 1 John 2:17 (ESV) says, "The world is passing away along with its desires, but whoever does the will of God abides forever."

I'm a grown-up, and I need to review this chapter again and again. It's hard. Life fights us on this like crazy, with so much work to be done and so many activities and people and social media updates demanding our attention! But it's a battle worth fighting to keep your time prioritized with the things that are most important.

And don't forget that resting matters to Jesus. God created a whole day for it!

*So God blessed the seventh day and made it holy,*
*because on it God rested from all his work*
*that he had done in creation.*

GENESIS 2:3 ESV

Also, one of the Ten Commandments commands us to rest!

*"Six days you shall work, but on the*
*seventh day you shall rest."*

EXODUS 34:21 ESV

Here are some more verses about resting from the Bible:

*Then Jesus said, "Let's go off by ourselves*
*to a quiet place and rest awhile."*

MARK 6:31 NLT

• • • • • ••

*"Be still, and know that I am God."*

PSALM 46:10 ESV

• • • • • ••

*"Better to have one handful with quietness*
*than two handfuls with hard work*
*and chasing the wind."*

ECCLESIASTES 4:6 NLT

We need rest to recharge and be able to do the things God has created us to do and to share His love the way He wants us to and bring glory to Him. If we spend our time putting God first and asking for His help to plan our time, there will always be enough time, and we will always find rest because Jesus said, "If you are tired from carrying

118

heavy burdens, come to me and I will give you rest. Take the yoke I give you. Put it on your shoulders and learn from me. I am gentle and humble, and you will find rest. This yoke is easy to bear, and this burden is light" (Matthew 11:28–30 CEV).

## Write About It!

Do you make time in your busy day to talk with Jesus?

........................................................................................................................

........................................................................................................................

........................................................................................................................

........................................................................................................................

........................................................................................................................

........................................................................................................................

........................................................................................................................

........................................................................................................................

........................................................................................................................

........................................................................................................................

........................................................................................................................

........................................................................................................................

........................................................................................................................

........................................................................................................................

........................................................................................................................

........................................................................................................................

........................................................................................................................

........................................................................................................................

# IT ALL MATTERS TO JESUS

✿ How you spend your time matters to Jesus.

✿ Daily quiet time to pray matters to Jesus.

✿ Daily quiet time to read the Bible matters to Jesus.

✿ Daily quiet time to be still and listen for God matters to Jesus.

✿ Not being too busy matters to Jesus.

✿ Taking time to rest matters to Jesus.

✿ Balancing our activities with time to spend with God matters to Jesus.

✿ .....................................................................................................

✿ .....................................................................................................

✿ .....................................................................................................

✿ .....................................................................................................

✿ .....................................................................................................

✿ .....................................................................................................

✿ .....................................................................................................

✿ .....................................................................................................

✿ .....................................................................................................

✿ .....................................................................................................

✿ .....................................................................................................

✿ .....................................................................................................

# Write About It!

Are you pleasing God with how you choose to spend your time?

........................................................................................

........................................................................................

........................................................................................

........................................................................................

........................................................................................

........................................................................................

........................................................................................

........................................................................................

........................................................................................

........................................................................................

........................................................................................

........................................................................................

........................................................................................

........................................................................................

........................................................................................

........................................................................................

........................................................................................

........................................................................................

........................................................................................

........................................................................................

........................................................................................

........................................................................................

# Joy, Joy, Joy!

These days, I can't hear the word *happy* without the fun tune from *Despicable Me 2* going through my mind, and then suddenly I'm dancing around like a crazy yellow minion. Anyone else with me on this? I love that movie!

What does it take to make you happy? You'll have a different answer to that question than your best friend or your sister or your cousin because every person is so different. *Happy* is so subjective, meaning what makes one person happy doesn't make another person happy in the same way. *Happy* is also kind of fickle, meaning it's not consistent and it changes pretty easily. Think about the things that made you *so* happy a few years ago. Would they make you happy in the same way now? Some things might, but as you grow up and mature it takes different things to make you happy.

Our culture puts a lot of importance on being happy. Maybe for school you've even memorized the famous line from our great nation's Declaration of Independence about "life, liberty, and the pursuit of happiness."

You'll often hear people say, "I just want to be happy," like that's the very best and brightest goal of life. And of course it's a wonderful thing to be happy, but if you pursue only happiness, you'll never stop chasing it—because you'll never be satisfied. And Jesus wants you to be satisfied. It matters to Him that you have *joy*, not just happiness, and that joy comes from Him.

Happiness is based on circumstances, and circumstances can change so easily. Think about how happy you are when your mom fixes your favorite food for supper. Then think about how unhappy you feel with a sick stomach if you eat way too much of the very thing that made you so happy at first.

Think about how happy you were when you received everything you asked for on your Christmas list when you were five years old. Now think about how unhappy those same gifts for Christmas might make you because you've grown up a lot since then.

Joy is based on Jesus, and He never changes. Joy is not just nice, upbeat feelings based on the good things going on around you; joy is a state of being content, confident, steady, and full of hope and positivity, even in the worst of circumstances. Joy comes from knowing Jesus as Savior and knowing that He wins against all the awful stuff that happens in this world, that He will conquer it all and one day we will live in perfect happiness with Him in heaven, forever!

Read these verses on joy, then thank Jesus and ask Him to fill you every day with His joy. It's a zillion times better than just being happy.

*Though you have not seen him, you love him; and*
*even though you do not see him now, you believe in*
*him and are filled with an inexpressible and glorious*
*joy, for you are receiving the end result of*
*your faith, the salvation of your souls.*

1 PETER 1:8–9 NIV

• • • • • • •

*A joyful heart is good medicine,*
*but a crushed spirit dries up the bones.*

PROVERBS 17:22 ESV

• • • • • • •

*So also you have sorrow now, but I will see you*
*again, and your hearts will rejoice, and no*
*one will take your joy from you.*

JOHN 16:22 ESV

*With all my heart, I will celebrate, and I can safely
rest. I am your chosen one. You won't leave me in the
grave or let my body decay. You have shown me the
path to life, and you make me glad by being near to
me. Sitting at your right side, I will always be joyful.*

PSALM 16:9–11 CEV

* * * * * * * *

*Dear brothers and sisters, when troubles of any kind
come your way, consider it an opportunity for great
joy. For you know that when your faith is tested, your
endurance has a chance to grow. So let it grow, for
when your endurance is fully developed, you will be
perfect and complete, needing nothing.*

JAMES 1:2–4 NLT

* * * * * * * *

*The hope of the righteous brings joy, but the
expectation of the wicked will perish.*

PROVERBS 10:28 ESV

* * * * * * * *

*Sing to the LORD, all you godly ones! Praise his holy
name. For his anger lasts only a moment, but his
favor lasts a lifetime! Weeping may last through the
night, but joy comes with the morning.*

PSALM 30:4–5 NLT

* * * * * * * *

*This is the day that the LORD has made;
let us rejoice and be glad in it.*

PSALM 118:24 ESV

*You make known to me the path of life; in your presence there is fullness of joy; at your right hand are pleasures forevermore.*

PSALM 16:11 ESV

· · · · · · ·

*May the God of hope fill you with all joy and peace as you trust in him, so that you may overflow with hope by the power of the Holy Spirit.*

ROMANS 15:13 NIV

## Write About It!

What brings you joy?

..............................................................................................

..............................................................................................

..............................................................................................

..............................................................................................

..............................................................................................

..............................................................................................

..............................................................................................

..............................................................................................

..............................................................................................

..............................................................................................

..............................................................................................

..............................................................................................

# IT ALL MATTERS TO JESUS

✿ Joy matters more than happiness to Jesus.

✿ Finding your joy in Him matters to Jesus.

✿ Praising God and singing with joy matters to Jesus.

✿ Sharing your joy with others matters to Jesus.

✿ ................................................................................................

✿ ................................................................................................

✿ ................................................................................................

✿ ................................................................................................

✿ ................................................................................................

✿ ................................................................................................

✿ ................................................................................................

✿ ................................................................................................

✿ ................................................................................................

✿ ................................................................................................

✿ ................................................................................................

✿ ................................................................................................

✿ ................................................................................................

✿ ................................................................................................

✿ ................................................................................................

# A Tongue Twister:
## Practice Pleasant Patience

Someday you'll probably have your own car, and you might want to design your own license plate. When I was in eighth grade, I (obviously) didn't own a car, but I had a cool English teacher who gave us an assignment to design a license plate and then write about what it meant. I still remember mine because I was rather proud of it—I H8 2 W8. I thought I was pretty clever, and I totally meant what it said, "I hate to wait."

Lots of years later, I still hate to wait sometimes. More often than I'd like to admit, in fact. But patience is one of the fruits of the Spirit. It should be plain to see in our lives if we've accepted the Holy Spirit, and it matters to Jesus if we practice patience.

How are you at waiting and being patient? Maybe there are some things you are fine waiting on. I'm always amazed that some people actually *enjoy* the wait in long lines at amusement parks or at stores for Black Friday shopping.

But there are all sorts of things that can make you feel impatient. Do your siblings take too much time in the bathroom in the mornings? Does Mom always seem to be forever cooking supper when your stomach is about to cave in from starvation? Do the minutes of the school day sometimes tick by in super slow motion? Does the countdown to summer break take an absolute eternity?

What's your attitude while you wait for these things? Does it need an adjustment? Do you stay calm and kind, or do you start to complain and freak out and get irritable and whiny?

And how do you feel when people are impatient with you? It's not fun, is it? But what about when others show you patience? That's nice, right? So, just like the Golden Rule says to "do unto others," you need to treat others with the patience that you know is nice to receive. It's hard, believe me I know, but it's the right thing to do.

Maybe there are big things that make you feel impatient. Have you been praying for what seems like forever for a parent to find a new job? Or for a relative to be healed from cancer? Or for a bully to leave you alone?

In all the ways that need your patience, hang in there. Ask God to keep you cool when impatience threatens to overheat your temper or cause you to doubt Him or make you want to give up. Check out these verses to help you stay focused and able to practice pleasant patience. (Can you say that out loud? It's quite a tongue twister!)

*My friends, be patient until the Lord returns. Think of farmers who wait patiently for the spring and summer rains to make their valuable crops grow. Be patient like those farmers and don't give up. The Lord will soon be here!*

JAMES 5:7–8 CEV

. . . . . . .

*Rejoice in our confident hope. Be patient in trouble, and keep on praying.*

ROMANS 12:12 NLT

. . . . . . .

*Be patient with everyone.*

1 THESSALONIANS 5:14 CEV

. . . . . . .

*Patience is better than pride.*

ECCLESIASTES 7:8 NLT

*If we look forward to something we don't yet have, we must wait patiently and confidently.*

ROMANS 8:25 NLT

• • • • • • •

*He will give eternal life to everyone who has patiently done what is good in the hope of receiving glory, honor, and life that lasts forever.*

ROMANS 2:7 CEV

• • • • • • •

*The LORD is kind to everyone who trusts and obeys him. It is good to wait patiently for the LORD to save us.*

LAMENTATIONS 3:25–26 CEV

• • • • • • •

*Be patient and trust the LORD. Don't let it bother you when all goes well for those who do sinful things.*

PSALM 37:7 CEV

• • • • • • •

*Patiently put up with each other  and love each other.*

EPHESIANS 4:2 CEV

• • • • • • •

*But they who wait for the LORD shall renew their strength; they shall mount up with wings like eagles; they shall run and not be weary; they shall walk and not faint.*

ISAIAH 40:31 ESV

*A servant of the Lord must not quarrel but must
be kind to everyone, be able to teach, and be
patient with difficult people.*

2 Timothy 2:24 nlt

• • • • • • •

*God loves you and has chosen you as his own special
people. So be gentle, kind, humble, meek, and patient.*

Colossians 3:12 cev

## Why is waiting so hard?

.................................................................................................

.................................................................................................

.................................................................................................

.................................................................................................

.................................................................................................

.................................................................................................

.................................................................................................

.................................................................................................

.................................................................................................

.................................................................................................

.................................................................................................

.................................................................................................

.................................................................................................

# IT ALL MATTERS TO JESUS

❀ Learning to be patient matters to Jesus.

❀ Having a good attitude while you're waiting matters to Jesus.

❀ Having patience with other people matters to Jesus.

❀ Letting God teach you while you're waiting on an answer to prayer matters to Jesus.

❀ Learning to trust God while you wait matters to Jesus.

❀ ......................................................................................

❀ ......................................................................................

❀ ......................................................................................

❀ ......................................................................................

❀ ......................................................................................

❀ ......................................................................................

❀ ......................................................................................

❀ ......................................................................................

❀ ......................................................................................

❀ ......................................................................................

❀ ......................................................................................

❀ ......................................................................................

❀ ......................................................................................

❀ ......................................................................................

# Write About It!

Are you waiting on an answer to prayer?
Write down the prayers you need extra patience for here.

# Peace Out

What are some of the things you fight most about with your siblings? I have two big brothers who used to sit on me when I tried to get the remote for the TV, and my sister and I fought over toys and clothes and who got to ride in the front seat of the car. I bet those kinds of fights with siblings are still pretty common today. Can you relate? Or maybe you sometimes fight with your friends over choosing what movie to watch or what game to play or activity to do. Or with your parents over chores or getting your homework done on time.

Here's a verse that talks about what causes fights:

> *Why do you fight and argue with each other?*
> *Isn't it because you are full of selfish desires*
> *that fight to control your body?*

JAMES 4:1 CEV

We are all full of selfish desires, and when we let them control us, then we usually end up in conflict with someone because eventually our selfish desire is going to clash with someone else's selfish desire.

For example, if there's one *last* of your mom's amazing chocolate chip cookies (or whatever treat you like best) sitting on a plate on the counter and you and your brother both reach for it at the same moment. . .suddenly you're shoving and yelling and wrestling and mad—all because of a cookie.

Or a selfish desire can clash with the rules and get you into conflict—like if you know it's your turn to let the dog out and feed him, but you just don't want to pause the movie you're watching to take care of him, so then the dog pees all over your sister's shoes and now your sister looks ready to pull all your hair out.

135

Or a selfish desire can clash with the requirements and get you into conflict—like if you blow off your history assignment because you just don't feel like doing it and you get an F and now your parents and teacher are less than thrilled with you and you're grounded and you're mad.

You get the idea.

Fighting is usually caused by people being selfish—and I know, I know, it's not always your fault or your selfishness that causes a fight. Sometimes the fights come to you. But whether you start conflict or not, you can always ask Jesus to help you *finish* it, because peace matters to Jesus.

Peace is a fruit of the Spirit (see Galatians 5:22), meaning it's something others can see in our lives when we've asked Jesus to be our Savior and have the Holy Spirit living in us. The Bible also says about peace:

*If possible, so far as it depends on you,*
*live peaceably with all.*

ROMANS 12:18 ESV

• • • • • • •

*Turn away from evil and do good.*
*Search for peace, and work to maintain it.*

1 PETER 3:11 NLT

• • • • • • •

*God blesses those who work for peace,*
*for they will be called the children of God.*

MATTHEW 5:9 NLT

• • • • • • •

*And those who are peacemakers will plant seeds of*
*peace and reap a harvest of righteousness.*

JAMES 3:18 NLT

*Work at living in peace with everyone, and*
*work at living a holy life, for those who are not*
*holy will not see the Lord.*

HEBREWS 12:14 NLT

• • • • • • •

*Those who plan peace have joy.*

PROVERBS 12:20 ESV

Being a peacemaker doesn't mean you have to be a wimp or let yourself be bullied when a fight comes to you that you didn't start. But it means that you do your part to make things right and peaceful. Here are some verses on how to make up when you're in the middle of a fight:

*Be kind to one another, tenderhearted, forgiving one*
*another, as God in Christ forgave you.*

EPHESIANS 4:32 ESV

• • • • • • •

*Put up with each other, and forgive anyone who does*
*you wrong, just as Christ has forgiven you. Love is*
*more important than anything else. It is what ties*
*everything completely together.*

COLOSSIANS 3:13–14 CEV

• • • • • • •

*"If another believer sins against you, go privately and*
*point out the offense. If the other person listens and*
*confesses it, you have won that person back. But if you*
*are unsuccessful, take one or two others with you and*
*go back again, so that everything you say may be*

*confirmed by two or three witnesses. If the person*
*still refuses to listen, take your case to the church."*

MATTHEW 18:15–17 NLT

For the stuff that is unfair, the fights you didn't start, the injustice that's been done to you, the stuff you just can't seem to get closure or a peaceful conclusion to, you leave that up to God. God is not some weak and wimpy old man in the sky. He is a righteous, holy, and just God. He sees all and knows all, and when you are living your life to obey Him, He will fight for you, and He will make all things right for you—not always exactly when you want Him to, but He will do it exactly at the right time that is best for you.

*Ask God to bless everyone who mistreats you. Ask him*
*to bless them and not to curse them. When others are*
*happy, be happy with them, and when they are sad,*
*be sad. Be friendly with everyone. Don't be proud and*
*feel that you are smarter than others. Make friends*
*with ordinary people. Don't mistreat someone who*
*has mistreated you. But try to earn the respect of*
*others, and do your best to live at peace with everyone.*
*Dear friends, don't try to get even. Let God take*
*revenge. In the Scriptures the Lord says, "I am the*
*one to take revenge and pay them back."*

ROMANS 12:14–19 CEV

Strive to be a peacemaker, and let God do the fighting!

# Write About It!

How can you be a peacemaker today?

......................................................................................

......................................................................................

......................................................................................

......................................................................................

......................................................................................

......................................................................................

......................................................................................

......................................................................................

......................................................................................

......................................................................................

......................................................................................

......................................................................................

......................................................................................

......................................................................................

......................................................................................

......................................................................................

......................................................................................

......................................................................................

# IT ALL MATTERS TO JESUS

✿ Being a peacemaker matters to Jesus.

✿ Living in peace with others matters to Jesus.

✿ Controlling the selfishness that often causes fighting matters to Jesus.

✿ Trusting God to help you make peace matters to Jesus.

✿ Loving and forgiving matters to Jesus.

✿ Searching for peace and working hard to keep peace matters to Jesus.

✿ .............................................................................................

✿ .............................................................................................

✿ .............................................................................................

✿ .............................................................................................

✿ .............................................................................................

✿ .............................................................................................

✿ .............................................................................................

✿ .............................................................................................

✿ .............................................................................................

✿ .............................................................................................

✿ .............................................................................................

✿ .............................................................................................

✿ .............................................................................................

# Peace In

We've talked about keeping peace around you on the outside, now what about on the inside? It matters a lot to Jesus that you have perfect peace in your heart and mind. Do you ever feel overly anxious and worried about things? I don't mean just the usual worried about a test coming up or worried that you're going to be late to school one too many times. I'm talking about sick-to-your-stomach, keep-you-awake-at-night, all-the-time kind of worry. It seems like more and more people have what's called anxiety problems—you hear doctors on TV and in magazines and on blogs talk a lot about it these days.

Maybe it's not something you're dealing with at your age, but if not now, someday you might. I'm not trying to scare you. I just want to make sure you know one way, *the best way*, that you can fight anxiety and have peace—by asking for help from the God who made you and loves you more than anyone else and who is the God of all peace (see Isaiah 9:6 and Romans 15:33) and comfort (see 2 Corinthians 1:3).

God's power to help us with our anxiety is bigger and better than anything any medical professional here on earth can do. Let me be clear, I am not saying that medical help is never necessary for anxiety. It absolutely is sometimes. But for Christians who have the Holy Spirit, first God wants us to bring our anxiety problems to Him and let Him help. The Bible tells us so again and again:

> *You will keep in perfect peace all who trust in you,*
> *all whose thoughts are fixed on you! Trust in the Lord*
> *always, for the Lord God is the eternal Rock.*
>
> Isaiah 26:3–4 nlt

*Don't worry about anything, but pray about everything. With thankful hearts offer up your prayers and requests to God. Then, because you belong to Christ Jesus, God will bless you with peace that no one can completely understand. And this peace will control the way you think and feel.*

PHILIPPIANS 4:6–7 CEV

• • • • • • •

*And let the peace of Christ rule in your hearts.*

COLOSSIANS 3:15 ESV

• • • • • • •

*I tell you not to worry about your life. Don't worry about having something to eat, drink, or wear. Isn't life more than food or clothing? Look at the birds in the sky! They don't plant or harvest. They don't even store grain in barns. Yet your Father in heaven takes care of them. Aren't you worth more than birds? Can worry make you live longer? Why worry about clothes? Look how the wild flowers grow. They don't work hard to make their clothes. But I tell you that Solomon with all his wealth wasn't as well clothed as one of them. God gives such beauty to everything that grows in the fields, even though it is here today and thrown into a fire tomorrow. He will surely do even more for you! Why do you have such little faith? Don't worry and ask yourselves, "Will we have anything to eat? Will we have anything to drink? Will we have any clothes to wear?" Only people who don't know God are always worrying about such things. Your Father in heaven knows that you need all of these. But more than anything else, put God's work first and do what he wants. Then the other things will be yours as well.*

MATTHEW 6:25–33 CEV

• • • • • • •

*Don't worry about tomorrow. It will take care of itself. You have enough to worry about today.*

MATTHEW 6:34 CEV

• • • • • • •

*Those who love your instructions have great peace and do not stumble. I long for your rescue, LORD, so I have obeyed your commands. I have obeyed your laws, for I love them very much. Yes, I obey your commandments and laws because you know everything I do.*

PSALM 119:165–168 NLT

• • • • • • •

*"I have told you these things, so that in me you may have peace. In this world you will have trouble. But take heart! I have overcome the world."*

JOHN 16:33 NIV

• • • • • • •

*For God is not a God of confusion but of peace.*

1 CORINTHIANS 14:33 ESV

• • • • • • •

*In peace I will lie down and sleep, for you alone, O LORD, will keep me safe.*

PSALM 4:8 NLT

143

*Humble yourselves, therefore, under God's mighty
hand, that he may lift you up in due time. Cast all
your anxiety on him because he cares for you.*

1 PETER 5:6–7 NIV

• • • • • • •

*"Peace I leave with you; my peace I give you. I do not
give to you as the world gives. Do not let your
hearts be troubled and do not be afraid."*

JOHN 14:27 NIV

• • • • • • •

*You will walk safely and never stumble; you will rest
without a worry and sleep soundly. So don't be afraid
of sudden disasters or storms that strike those who
are evil. You can be sure that the LORD
will protect you from harm.*

PROVERBS 3:23–26 CEV

• • • • • • •

*My health may fail, and my spirit may
grow weak, but God remains the strength
of my heart; he is mine forever.*

PSALM 73:26 NLT

Whenever you might find yourself overwhelmed with worry and stress and anxiety, read these verses, memorize them, recite them over and over. Let Jesus, the Prince of Peace, calm you and steady you, and remember that someday soon we will live in peace with Him FOREVER without a worry or care ever again.

*"Do not let your hearts be troubled. You believe in
God; believe also in me. My Father's house has many*

*rooms; if that were not so, would I have told you that I am going there to prepare a place for you? And if I go and prepare a place for you, I will come back and take you to be with me that you also may be where I am."*

JOHN 14:1–3 NIV

 Write About It!

What kinds of things make you nervous?
What helps you to have inner peace?

........................................................................................

........................................................................................

........................................................................................

........................................................................................

........................................................................................

........................................................................................

........................................................................................

........................................................................................

........................................................................................

........................................................................................

........................................................................................

........................................................................................

........................................................................................

........................................................................................

# IT ALL MATTERS TO JESUS

- ❀ All your worries matter to Jesus.

- ❀ Giving you peace on the inside matters to Jesus.

- ❀ Being your peace matters to Jesus.

- ❀ Giving you peaceful sleep matters to Jesus.

- ❀ Helping you feel safe matters to Jesus.

- ❀ Letting God have power over your anxiety matters to Jesus.

- ❀ .............................................................................................

- ❀ .............................................................................................

- ❀ .............................................................................................

- ❀ .............................................................................................

- ❀ .............................................................................................

- ❀ .............................................................................................

- ❀ .............................................................................................

- ❀ .............................................................................................

- ❀ .............................................................................................

- ❀ .............................................................................................

- ❀ .............................................................................................

- ❀ .............................................................................................

- ❀ .............................................................................................

- ❀ .............................................................................................

# Don't Be a Meanie!

Have you ever gotten stuck in line at one of those self-checkout stations at the grocery store? I had an experience once where I was trying buy some fruit that wouldn't ring up correctly, and all of a sudden the machine was yelling at me over and over, "Move your Asian pears! Move your Asian pears!" in a loud robotic voice, with a line of customers behind me looking pretty grumpy. Um, can you say AWKWARD? Now that I look back, it's super funny though.

Ever since that experience, I remember it and laugh to myself when I'm stuck in line behind someone who's having a similar problem at the grocery story—and I act kindly toward them, even if it means I'm stuck in line a little longer. I smile and show them it's not a big deal if I have to wait a little extra while they get the problem figured out. I've been in their shoes before. I'll help if I can, and at the very least I'll be pleasant and not make the situation worse by being grumpy and rude.

I've noticed recently how unkind people can be while they wait in line at a busy store or in traffic, and it's so frustrating and just plain mean! Decide now while you're young not to be one of those people. Choose to be a person who shows kindness at every opportunity. Hold doors for people. Smile and be friendly. Go out of your way to help someone. If you see someone behind you in line who has just a couple of items and you have a whole cartful, let them go ahead of you. Wait for things patiently.

There are a zillion kind things you can do for others, and they don't have to be big things. Make a list of the little things you could do around the house or at school or when you're out and about that would show kindness to others.

One of the simplest ways to be kind is with encouragement. Have you ever been like Alexander having a terrible, horrible, no good, very bad day, but then just a simple, kind, and encouraging word helped change everything?

Maybe your teacher told you what a great job you did on your project or a friend complimented your outfit or your mom noticed how nicely you cleaned up your room and left you a thank-you note for it in your lunch box. It feels great, doesn't it? And it feels even better to be the giver of those kind words. To watch a person's face light up with a smile as they feel encouraged and appreciated is priceless! But it doesn't have to be in person. Just a simple email or text message to let someone know you're thinking of them and praying for them can mean so much to someone going through a rough time. Start the habit now of being a person who looks for the good in others and encourages them and thanks them for it.

And be sure to try this—even when you don't *feel* like being kind, be kind anyway and just watch how it changes you and those around you.

Kindness in both our actions and our words matters to Jesus. It's one of the fruits of the Spirit, which shows that we are true Christians.

*But the fruit of the Spirit is love, joy,*
*peace, patience, kindness, goodness,*
*faithfulness, gentleness, self-control.*

GALATIANS 5:22–23 ESV

The Bible also says all this about kindness:

*"But love your enemies, and do good, and lend,*
*expecting nothing in return, and your reward will*
*be great, and you will be sons of the Most High,*
*for he is kind to the ungrateful and the evil."*

LUKE 6:35 ESV

*Be kind to one another, tenderhearted, forgiving one
another, as God in Christ forgave you.*

EPHESIANS 4:32 ESV

• • • • • • •

*Your kindness will reward you,
but your cruelty will destroy you.*

PROVERBS 11:17 NLT

• • • • • • •

*Since God chose you to be the holy people he loves, you
must clothe yourselves with tenderhearted mercy,
kindness, humility, gentleness, and patience.*

COLOSSIANS 3:12 NLT

• • • • • • •

*Therefore, whenever we have the opportunity,
we should do good to everyone—especially to those
in the family of faith.*

GALATIANS 6:10 NLT

• • • • • • •

*Teach those who are rich in this world not to be proud
and not to trust in their money, which is so unreliable.
Their trust should be in God, who richly gives us all
we need for our enjoyment. Tell them to use their
money to do good. They should be rich in good works
and generous to those in need, always being ready to
share with others. By doing this they will be storing
up their treasure as a good foundation for the future
so that they may experience true life.*

1 TIMOTHY 6:17–19 NLT

*Dear brothers and sisters,*
*never get tired of doing good.*

2 Thessalonians 3:13 NLT

• • • • • • •

*We should help others do what is right*
*and build them up in the Lord.*

Romans 15:2 NLT

• • • • • • •

*Children, you show love for others by truly helping*
*them, and not merely by talking about it.*

1 John 3:18 CEV

In what ways can you spread kindness today?

# IT ALL MATTERS TO JESUS

- ❀ Being kind to others matters to Jesus.
- ❀ Encouraging others matters to Jesus.
- ❀ Holding doors for others matters to Jesus.
- ❀ Being polite to others matters to Jesus.
- ❀ Smiling at others matters to Jesus.
- ❀ Letting others go first matters to Jesus.
- ❀ Being kind even when you don't feel like it matters to Jesus.
- ❀ ............................................................................................
- ❀ ............................................................................................
- ❀ ............................................................................................
- ❀ ............................................................................................
- ❀ ............................................................................................
- ❀ ............................................................................................
- ❀ ............................................................................................
- ❀ ............................................................................................
- ❀ ............................................................................................
- ❀ ............................................................................................
- ❀ ............................................................................................
- ❀ ............................................................................................

# From Another World

Do you like the movie *Lilo and Stitch*? I love it! Poor Lilo is so funny and misunderstood, and Stitch is such a crazy but cute little alien guy. The lovely setting of Hawaii (even in cartoon form) is so nice to watch too. I think it would be amazing to live somewhere I could walk to beautiful sands and warm ocean waters. Ahhhh. . .

Anyway, back to aliens. Did you know that as a Christian you're supposed to be like an alien? I don't mean you're supposed to start growing extra eyeballs or turn green or start communicating with clicks and screeches through baby monitors.

I mean *alien* as in *a stranger* like this definition from *Merriam-Webster*: "belonging or relating to another person, place, or thing."

And like this verse of the Bible that uses the word *alien*: "Dear friends, I urge you, as aliens and strangers in the world, to abstain from sinful desires, which war against your soul. Live such good lives among the pagans that, though they accuse you of doing wrong, they may see your good deeds and glorify God on the day he visits us" (1 Peter 2:11 NIV, 1984).

Basically, as someone who loves and follows Jesus, you are supposed to be an alien, a foreigner, or a stranger to this world because you know that you are just here on this earth for a short time compared to where you ultimately belong—with God in heaven forever. But while you're here, the things you do differently than the world, the strange "alien" ways about you, will show others that you follow and worship the one, true God.

It means when most people in the world are looking out for themselves, you're looking out for others first.

It means when most people in the world say it's okay to cheat and lie a little, you're being honest.

It means when most people in the world are turning away from the Bible, you're sticking to it.

It means when most people in the world think going to church is a waste of time, you keep on going.

It means when most people in the world say any type of TV or movies are okay, you are careful what you watch.

It means when most people in the world say there is no God, you keep living for Him.

It means that compared to most people in the world, the people around you see real differences in the way you live your life.

It means you strive to do everything with excellence because everything you do is for God:

> *But since you excel in everything—in faith, in speech, in knowledge, in complete earnestness and in the love we have kindled in you—see that you also excel in this grace of giving.*
>
> 2 CORINTHIANS 8:7 NIV

• • • • • • •

> *Work with enthusiasm, as though you were working for the Lord rather than for people. Remember that the Lord will reward each one of us for the good we do.*
>
> EPHESIANS 6:7–8 NLT

• • • • • • •

> *By his divine power, God has given us everything we need for living a godly life. We have received all of this by coming to know him, the one who called us to himself by means of his marvelous glory and excellence. And because of his glory and excellence, he has given us great and precious promises. These*

*are the promises that enable you to share his divine*
*nature and escape the world's corruption*
*caused by human desires.*

*In view of all this, make every effort to respond*
*to God's promises. Supplement your faith with a*
*generous provision of moral excellence, and moral*
*excellence with knowledge, and knowledge with self-*
*control, and self-control with patient endurance, and*
*patient endurance with godliness, and godliness*
*with brotherly affection, and brotherly*
*affection with love for everyone.*

2 Peter 1:3–7 nlt

It means you strive to do everything with integrity:

*Whoever walks in integrity walks securely, but he*
*who makes his ways crooked will be found out.*

Proverbs 10:9 esv

. . . . . . . .

*Better is a poor man who walks in his integrity*
*than a rich man who is crooked in his ways.*

Proverbs 28:6 esv

. . . . . . . .

*If you do the right thing, honesty will be your guide.*
*But if you are crooked, you will be trapped*
*by your own dishonesty.*

Proverbs 11:3 cev

*Better is a poor person who walks in his integrity*
*than one who is crooked in speech and is a fool.*

PROVERBS 19:1 ESV

• • • • • • •

*Show yourself in all respects to be*
*a model of good works.*

TITUS 2:7 ESV

And it means you strive to live a holy life:

*Be alert and think straight. Put all your hope in how*
*kind God will be to you when Jesus Christ appears.*
*Behave like obedient children. Don't let your lives be*
*controlled by your desires, as they used to be. Always*
*live as God's holy people should, because God is the*
*one who chose you, and he is holy. That's why*
*the Scriptures say, "I am the holy God,*
*and you must be holy too."*

1 PETER 1:13–16 CEV

• • • • • • •

*We should stay away from everything that keeps our*
*bodies and spirits from being clean. We should honor*
*God and try to be completely like him.*

2 CORINTHIANS 7:1 CEV

• • • • • • •

*Work at living in peace with everyone,*
*and work at living a holy life, for those who*
*are not holy will not see the Lord.*

HEBREWS 12:14 NLT

*You are God's chosen and special people. You are a group of royal priests and a holy nation. God has brought you out of darkness into his marvelous light.*

1 PETER 2:9 CEV

• • • • • • •

*God has called us to live holy lives, not impure lives.*

1 THESSALONIANS 4:7 NLT

• • • • • • •

*In a wealthy home some utensils are made of gold and silver, and some are made of wood and clay. The expensive utensils are used for special occasions, and the cheap ones are for everyday use. If you keep yourself pure, you will be a special utensil for honorable use. Your life will be clean, and you will be ready for the Master to use you for every good work.*

2 TIMOTHY 2:20–21 NLT

• • • • • • •

*May the God of peace make you holy in every way, and may your whole spirit and soul and body be kept blameless until our Lord Jesus Christ comes again.*

1 THESSALONIANS 5:23 NLT

So embrace your "inner alien" and be so different from the world that others see that difference and want to know more about Jesus too!

## Write About It!

How do you stand apart from the world?

........................................................................................

........................................................................................

........................................................................................

........................................................................................

........................................................................................

........................................................................................

........................................................................................

........................................................................................

........................................................................................

........................................................................................

........................................................................................

........................................................................................

........................................................................................

........................................................................................

........................................................................................

........................................................................................

........................................................................................

........................................................................................

........................................................................................

........................................................................................

........................................................................................

# IT ALL MATTERS TO JESUS

- Being very different from the world matters to Jesus.

- Being honest when others are lying matters to Jesus.

- Reading the Bible when others have stopped matters to Jesus.

- Going to church when so many don't anymore matters to Jesus.

- Living a holy life matters to Jesus.

- Being careful what you watch and listen to and read matters to Jesus.

- Having integrity matters to Jesus.

- ................................................................................

- ................................................................................

- ................................................................................

- ................................................................................

- ................................................................................

- ................................................................................

- ................................................................................

- ................................................................................

- ................................................................................

- ................................................................................

- ................................................................................

# Write About It!

Has anyone ever asked why you seem different?
If so, what did you say?

# Don't Eat *All* the Chocolate

I have a hard time around chocolate. It's *soooooo* good that I forget not to eat too much sometimes. Okay, *a lot* of the time! Do you have a favorite food you go crazy for? Is it candy or chips or pizza or something else? But what happens if you eat way too much of that favorite food? Sometimes the result is not pretty. We have to control how much we eat at one time or we get sick. Self-control matters for a lot of things in our lives, not just food.

For example, how much TV should you watch?

How much time should you spend on the computer?

How much time should you spend on the phone with your friends?

How much time do you need to spend on your homework?

How much time do you need to do your chores?

How much time do you need to sleep at night?

How much time do you need to spend being active and getting exercise rather than just chilling on the couch?

All these things need self-control to manage the hours in the day and the things you need to do to be healthy and meet your responsibilities.

You also need self-control over your tongue—the things you say.

*Watching what you say can save you a lot of trouble.*

PROVERBS 21:23 CEV

And you need self-control over your emotions and reactions.

*My dear friends, you should be quick to listen and
slow to speak or to get angry.*

JAMES 1:19 CEV

And you need self-control over your thoughts.

*Finally, my friends, keep your minds on whatever is true, pure, right, holy, friendly, and proper. Don't ever stop thinking about what is truly worthwhile and worthy of praise.*

PHILIPPIANS 4:8 CEV

When you're young, you're still learning a lot about self-control, and hopefully a grown-up is helping you figure it out, but each year you get older, you're more and more responsible. And don't ever forget that you're never alone. The Holy Spirit is with you and will help you keep control. Just ask Him!

Read and think about these verses to help you!

*A person without self-control is like a city with broken-down walls.*

PROVERBS 25:28 NLT

• • • • • • •

*Do your best to improve your faith. You can do this by adding goodness, understanding, self-control, patience, devotion to God, concern for others, and love.*

2 PETER 1:5–7 CEV

• • • • • • •

*Be self-controlled and sober-minded for the sake of your prayers.*

1 PETER 4:7 ESV

*For God gave us a spirit not of fear but of*
*power and love and self-control.*

2 TIMOTHY 1:7 ESV

Why is having self-control important?

........................................................................................

........................................................................................

........................................................................................

........................................................................................

........................................................................................

........................................................................................

........................................................................................

........................................................................................

........................................................................................

........................................................................................

........................................................................................

........................................................................................

........................................................................................

........................................................................................

........................................................................................

........................................................................................

........................................................................................

........................................................................................

# IT ALL MATTERS TO JESUS

- ✿ Self-control matters to Jesus.

- ✿ Being careful what you say matters to Jesus.

- ✿ Eating healthy foods in healthy ways matters to Jesus.

- ✿ Having enough time for schoolwork matters to Jesus.

- ✿ Getting enough sleep at night matters to Jesus.

- ✿ Exercising your body in a healthy way matters to Jesus.

- ✿ Making time to help with chores matters to Jesus.

- ✿ Having control over your tongue matters to Jesus.

- ✿ Having control over your thoughts matters to Jesus.

- ✿ ......................................................................................................

- ✿ ......................................................................................................

- ✿ ......................................................................................................

- ✿ ......................................................................................................

- ✿ ......................................................................................................

- ✿ ......................................................................................................

- ✿ ......................................................................................................

- ✿ ......................................................................................................

- ✿ ......................................................................................................

- ✿ ......................................................................................................

# Strengths and Weaknesses

I remember when I was in the third grade, I told some friends I was going to be a superstar gymnast and get all the way to the Olympics—the problem was I'd never had any lessons, and other than being able to do splits and cartwheels okay, I was not really any good at gymnastics. I sure needed a reality check! LOL!

I eventually figured out that my dream of being an Olympic gymnast just wasn't going to happen for me, and that was okay. Gymnastics was not a strength God had given me. What He had given me was a gift for reading and writing and learning, and I began to focus on what I could do with that. I started dreaming of working for a Christian publishing company, and now I do exactly what I dreamed of!

Maybe gymnastics is something *you* are great at. Or soccer or dance or running or drawing or music or public speaking or making new friends or whatever!

God has given you a unique set of strengths and talents, and it matters that you figure out what they are and then use them for God, doing your very best at them as a way to praise and worship Him! Do you know that praise and worship doesn't mean just singing time at church? Praise and worship can be anything you do that pleases God and gives Him the glory. It's a way of life—giving your life to God and living your life for God, in a way that everything you do tries to honor Him.

*And so, dear brothers and sisters, I plead with you to give your bodies to God because of all he has done for you. Let them be a living and holy sacrifice— the kind he will find acceptable. This is truly the way to worship him.*

Romans 12:1 NLT

165

Strengths aren't just the activities and hobbies and sports we're good at. We've all been given spiritual gifts too.

*Each of you has been blessed with one of God's many wonderful gifts to be used in the service of others. So use your gift well. If you have the gift of speaking, preach God's message. If you have the gift of helping others, do it with the strength that God supplies. Everything should be done in a way that will bring honor to God because of Jesus Christ, who is glorious and powerful forever.*

1 PETER 4:10–11 CEV

• • • • • • •

*In his grace, God has given us different gifts for doing certain things well. So if God has given you the ability to prophesy, speak out with as much faith as God has given you. If your gift is serving others, serve them well. If you are a teacher, teach well. If your gift is to encourage others, be encouraging. If it is giving, give generously. If God has given you leadership ability, take the responsibility seriously. And if you have a gift for showing kindness to others, do it gladly.*

ROMANS 12:6–8 NLT

Just like everyone has strengths, that means the opposite is true—everyone has weaknesses. But do you know weaknesses don't have to be a bad thing? The Bible says that when we are weak, we are strong. That's kind of confusing, huh? Like a paradox.

Here's the scripture that comes from:

*Three times I begged the Lord to make this suffering go away. But he replied, "My kindness is all you need. My power is strongest when you are weak." So if Christ keeps giving me his power, I will gladly brag about how weak I am. Yes, I am glad to be weak or insulted or mistreated or to have troubles and sufferings, if it is for Christ. Because when I am weak, I am strong.*

2 CORINTHIANS 12:8–10 CEV

It means that the things we are weak at are what make us depend on God more. We need His help more with the things we're not good at, so we ask Him more and lean on Him more, and in the end that makes us stronger—because it's far better to be completely weak and dependent on God than it is to focus only on our strength and depend on just ourselves.

So, figure out your strengths and don't be frustrated by your weaknesses. Use both of them to worship God and let Him shine in your life!

## What are your strengths?

..................................................................................................................

..................................................................................................................

..................................................................................................................

..................................................................................................................

..................................................................................................................

..................................................................................................................

# IT ALL MATTERS TO JESUS

- ❀ Your strengths matter to Jesus.
- ❀ Your weaknesses matter to Jesus.
- ❀ Using your strengths for God matters to Jesus.
- ❀ Letting God help you in your weaknesses matters to Jesus.
- ❀ ......................................................................................
- ❀ ......................................................................................
- ❀ ......................................................................................
- ❀ ......................................................................................
- ❀ ......................................................................................
- ❀ ......................................................................................
- ❀ ......................................................................................
- ❀ ......................................................................................
- ❀ ......................................................................................
- ❀ ......................................................................................
- ❀ ......................................................................................
- ❀ ......................................................................................
- ❀ ......................................................................................
- ❀ ......................................................................................
- ❀ ......................................................................................
- ❀ ......................................................................................

## Write About It!

What are your weaknesses?

_____

_____

_____

_____

_____

_____

_____

_____

_____

_____

_____

_____

_____

_____

_____

_____

_____

_____

_____

_____

# Constant Conversation

Are you quiet in general, or are you mostly a talker? Or does it depend on where you're at and who you're with? Maybe you're quiet at school or church or in a group, but at home or one-on-one with someone, you could talk all day.

Whom do you love to talk to the most? Your BFF or a family member? Or maybe even your pet? My dog is fun to talk to. He's a good listener and cocks his head so cute just like he's trying to understand.

Do you know who the best listener is and who's always available and who wishes you'd never stop talking to Him? You've probably guessed it! God. And while He was here on earth, Jesus taught about how we should pray because it matters so much to Him that we communicate regularly, constantly with Him!

Here is the Lord's Prayer, which is probably familiar to you, but maybe not in this version:

> *"When you pray, don't be like those show-offs who love to stand up and pray in the meeting places and on the street corners. They do this just to look good. I can assure you that they already have their reward. When you pray, go into a room alone and close the door. Pray to your Father in private. He knows what is done in private, and he will reward you.*
>
> *When you pray, don't talk on and on as people do who don't know God. They think God likes to hear long prayers. Don't be like them. Your Father knows what you need before you ask. You should pray like this:*

*'Our Father in heaven, help us to honor your name.*
*Come and set up your kingdom, so that everyone on*
*earth will obey you, as you are obeyed in heaven.*
*Give us our food for today. Forgive us for doing*
*wrong, as we forgive others. Keep us from*
*being tempted and protect us from evil.' "*

MATTHEW 6:5–13 CEV

This is a model of prayer that Jesus gave us, showing us how to pray sincerely, with praise and honor to God, asking that His will be done first and foremost, asking for just what we need for each day, asking for forgiveness of sins and help to forgive others, and asking for protection against sin and against evil.

So, is this the only prayer we should ever say, and just recite it word for word? Should we not have specific prayer requests for specific people and problems? No, that's not what this means because the Bible also tells us other ways to pray.

The Bible tells us to pray for our salvation and for others to be saved too:

*Please, LORD, please save us.*
*Please, LORD, please give us success.*

PSALM 118:25 NLT

• • • • • • •

*Dear friends, my greatest wish and my prayer to God*
*is for the people of Israel to be saved.*

ROMANS 10:1 CEV

The Bible says not to worry about anything, but to tell God all of our needs:

*Don't worry about anything, but pray about*
*everything. With thankful hearts offer up your*
*prayers and requests to God. Then, because you*
*belong to Christ Jesus, God will bless you with peace*
*that no one can completely understand. And this*
*peace will control the way you think and feel.*

PHILIPPIANS 4:6–7 CEV

The Bible tells us to pray for others:

*First of all, I ask you to pray for everyone. Ask God*
*to help and bless them all, and tell God how thankful*
*you are for each of them. Pray for kings and others in*
*power, so that we may live quiet and peaceful lives as*
*we worship and honor God. This kind of*
*prayer is good, and it pleases God our Savior.*
*God wants everyone to be saved.*

1 TIMOTHY 2:1–4 CEV

· · · · · · ·

*Therefore, confess your sins to each other and pray*
*for each other so that you may be healed. The prayer*
*of a righteous person is powerful and effective.*

JAMES 5:16 NIV

The Bible tells us to pray for wisdom:

*If any of you need wisdom, you should ask God,*
*and it will be given to you. God is generous*
*and won't correct you for asking.*

JAMES 1:5 CEV

You can pray anywhere anytime because God is always with you through the Holy Spirit, and even when you don't know what to pray for, pray anyway because:

*In certain ways we are weak, but the Spirit is here to help us. For example, when we don't know what to pray for, the Spirit prays for us in ways that cannot be put into words. All of our thoughts are known to God. He can understand what is in the mind of the Spirit, as the Spirit prays for God's people.*

ROMANS 8:26–27 CEV

Most importantly, don't ever stop praying. Keep in constant communication with God so that He can help you with each and every moment, because it all matters to Him!

*Never stop praying.*

1 THESSALONIANS 5:17 CEV

How much time do you spend talking to God?
Why is talking to Him so important?

.................................................................................................

.................................................................................................

.................................................................................................

.................................................................................................

.................................................................................................

# IT ALL MATTERS TO JESUS

❀ Praying without bragging about it matters to Jesus.

❀ Praying for God's will matters to Jesus.

❀ Praying for others matters to Jesus.

❀ Praying for wisdom matters to Jesus.

❀ Sharing all your needs and worries and requests with God in prayer matters to Jesus.

❀ Constantly praying matters to Jesus.

❀ ...............................................................................................

❀ ...............................................................................................

❀ ...............................................................................................

❀ ...............................................................................................

❀ ...............................................................................................

❀ ...............................................................................................

❀ ...............................................................................................

❀ ...............................................................................................

❀ ...............................................................................................

❀ ...............................................................................................

❀ ...............................................................................................

❀ ...............................................................................................